SIMPLY MINDFUL MEAL BY MEAL

101 MINDFUL WAYS TO CREATE A HEALTHY RELATIONSHIP WITH FOOD

SIMPLY MINDFUL BOOK SERIES

DONALD ALTMAN

SIMPLY MINDFUL MEAL BY MEAL

The information in this book is meant only for educational purposes and not as a substitute for mental health professional care, nutritional, dietary or medical advice. No implied or expressed guarantee regarding the effects of these recommendations or practices can be given, and no liability assumed.

ABOUT THE AUTHOR

Donald Altman, MA, LPC, is a psychotherapist, award-winning author, and former Buddhist monk. Featured in *The Mindfulness Movie* and profiled in *The Living Spiritual Teachers Project*, he has written over 20 books that teach how to incorporate mindfulness into daily life. Donald conducts mindfulness workshops and retreats internationally and has trained over 15,000 mental health therapists and healthcare professionals on how to use mindfulness as a tool for managing depression, anxiety, pain and stress.

Donald served as vice-president of The Center for Mindful Eating and as an adjunct professor in Portland State University's Interpersonal Neurobiology Certificate Program and at Lewis and Clark Graduate School of Education and Counseling. He travels internationally, spreading seeds of mindfulness as a health and business consultant, keynote speaker, and mindfulness workshop leader.

Donald's first novel, *Travelers*, was a 2023 Next Generation Indie Book Awards recipient. *Travelers* is a spiritual adventure about a psychiatrist who is forced to take a mystical journey in order to save a young patient in the psych ward, as well as save his marriage and life after a devastating personal loss.

Donald lives in Portland, Oregon, enjoying the beauty and awe of nature with his beloved wife, family and friends.

mindfulpractices.com

facebook.com/mndfulpractices

ACKNOWLEDGMENTS

The book is possible because of the teachers, students, spiritual friends and other encouragers who have accompanied me on my mindfulness journey. For all those who I have met in workshops or online, thank you for sharing your spirit, life experiences and inspiration.

I will always be thankful for the teachings of the Venerable U. Silananda, my friend Lama Surya Das, and my spiritual brother and devoted Buddhist scholar U. Thitzana. Thanks to editor and friend John Nelson for sharing editorial feedback, levity and creativity. I am very grateful for the kind support of John Arden and Supatra Tovar, who took time to read the manuscript and provide inspiring insights on the back cover. Gratitude to Bruce Hanson, a friend and artist whose design flair enhanced the cover. Thanks also to Randy Fitzgerald and Gabe Lee. I am especially indebted to my mother Barbara, a shining light and spiritual guide in my life.

Finally, I bow with gratitude to my beloved *Ba'ku del cuore* Maria, a soul friend and life partner, for offering a cornucopia of contributions, editorial and otherwise, all the while dancing with me to the tune of the possible and beautiful.

Travelers all, on this blue planet—
May we find our true purpose
by helping those travelers
we encounter each day,
in ways both large and small.
And, as an ancient blessing advises—
'May suffering ones be suffering free,
May the fear struck fearless be,
May grieving ones shed all grief,
May all beings find relief.'
And as we awaken,
May we all travel in peace.

TABLE OF CONTENTS

Step 1: Entry, Hunger and Choices

Step 2: Preparation and Ritual

Step 4: Departure

INTRODUCTION

How can anyone develop a mindful relationship with food? This is one of those elusive concepts that everyone talks about—but is best understood through practice. I have always been amazed at how food serves as a powerful healing medium for those who struggle with it. Having faced my own share of mindless and emotional eating, as well as having seen the benefits of mindfulness when working as a senior mental health therapist in an eating disorder clinic, it is my honor to share with you the daily mindful eating practices in these pages.

Simply Mindful Meal by Meal offers 101 detailed tools, practices and meditations for cultivating mealtime mindfulness.

These diverse practices include everything from personal inventories to guided reflections and meditations based on the healing and ancient path of mindfulness. For these reasons, the goal of this book is simple and direct:

Instead of fearing, obsessing or mindlessly consuming food, you will learn how to cultivate a healthy and peaceful relationship to food, body and eating.

THE 4-STEP FOOD JOURNEY

Simply Mindful Meal by Meal is organized in four sections, which I refer to as the "4-Step Food Journey." These steps are so natural that you may not have consciously considered them—even though you experience these each time you eat. They include: 1) *entry into the meal*, 2) *meal preparation*, 3) *eating the meal* and 4) *departing from the meal.*

While the steps may seem obvious, your experience of each changes dramatically once mindful awareness is added to the mix. Mindful eating infuses you with awakened compassion, as well as a new and deeper understanding of your relationship to each morsel and the world around you.

Let's look a little more closely at the 4-Step Food Journey so you'll better understand how to use these practices and what to expect.

Step 1: *Entry, Hunger and Choices* examines the level of hunger and emotions you carry into each meal. What is the emotional energy you bring with you to today's meal? Are you excited to gain sustenance and meaning? Are you tired and worn out, just going through the motions of eating? Are you emotionally upset as you sit down to eat? Also, what is the level of your hunger? Are you starved, or maybe not hungry at all, but just eating socially or out of habit? All these factors affect what you choose to eat, how fast you eat, and how you feel after the meal, including your emotional, mental and physical states. That's a lot to consider, isn't it?!

This section also shines light on your body's energy needs. When does your body require more food, or less? What *kind* of nourishment does your body truly desire at this moment? *Simply Mindful Meal by Meal* will serve as a guide to help you make better decisions and go beyond ingrained and harmful habitual choices.

Most importantly, the practices here focus on small, achievable steps that you can take today. Even if you make a simple change, such as not eating emotionally or taking one conscious bite of a food that is beneficial for you, that is measurable progress. Once you know your hunger level and what your body is actually hungry for, you won't need to eat because of "what's eating you." How liberating!

Step 2: *Preparation and Ritual* looks at how to be mindful of even the simplest of tasks. Cleaning the kitchen, for example, can be viewed either as an onerous chore or as a way to cleanse and beautify. The meditations and practices in this section encourage you to watch your thoughts and attitudes as you prepare the kitchen for your meal. Or, if you're eating at a restaurant, preparation can include everything from the route you take to arrive at the restaurant to how you move and walk into the space, as well as how you relate to others.

Rituals are integral to this section because they serve to enhance your awareness of the miracle of food to sustain life. When you eat for emotional reasons or out of boredom, it may be a sign that you seek greater meaning in your meals—and your life. Mealtime rituals offer such fulfillment. Rituals are also very personal in how you decide to enact them. You might pause for a moment to say grace or a blessing before each meal, or you might just take a deep breath and a moment of silence to appreciate everyone and everything that made this food possible.

Step 3: *Eating and Community* shares tools for helping you eat with presence, patience and in moderation. Even the Buddha, for instance, experienced extremes with food. As a prince he ate to excess; as an ascetic he starved himself. Neither approach worked. It was only after eating a moderate meal that he attained enlightenment. And so, he learned the "middle way" of moderation that led to peace and liberation from suffering.

If you have found moderation to be difficult, you are not alone. And so, it can be useful to ask, what does it mean to have patience and moderation with food? Instead of blaming yourself for how you are eating, you can take a moment's pause between bites by taking a conscious breath. For example, you can mentally think "Creating a breath" as you slowly breathe in; you can think "ending a breath" as you gently exhale. Do this and give yourself the gift of moderation and patience . . . if only for a few seconds. During the years that I worked as a therapist at an eating disorder clinic, I often ate meals with the patients. They liked a minute of conscious breathing before eating because it helped them quiet their minds, lessen their fears, and be more accepting and moderate in their approach to food.

Awareness of the community that surrounds us is also relevant to mealtime. While eating, we can be mindful of how each food connects us to the planet and community. Each meal, each morsel is a gift. That is why—even if you are single and eat many meals by yourself—each meal brings you into communion with the community at large.

Consider how the Earth, the sun and the rain clouds provide a bounty of food. Farmers plant seeds and harvest crops. Truckers transport food to distribution centers. Retailers stock the shelves. This great chain of giving and receiving never sleeps. In the broader sense, is not each meal—indeed, everything in your life—something that is given?

Step 4: *Departure* looks at how to transition from mealtime and be at peace with the meal you have just eaten. As one meal ends, another journey begins. What energy fills your body after your meal? Are you drowsy? Alert? Anxious? Guilty? Upset? Angry? The tools and ideas in this section will help you pay greater attention to how different foods affect your body and digestion. You'll also become more skillful at moving forward to your "after meal" activities with a greater sense of ease, peace and grace.

USING THE PRACTICES

To get the most out of each practice or meditation, find a quiet space where you can spend a minute reading the quotation and commentary or story that precedes the meditation. Gently take a slow, satisfying breath as you read the commentary, reflecting on what this means for you and the upcoming meal.

After sitting a moment longer, read through the **Practice/Meditation** section that follows. Read slowly and take your time to absorb it. Here you will find all the detailed steps needed to help you reflect or act upon the ideas in the practice. As you follow the guided practice, you might even imagine that these are wise words you have written to yourself. If you are alone, you could even softly whisper them to yourself as a kind, caring and nurturing friend might.

Remember that you eat thousands of meals in a lifetime. *There is no perfect meal for you. There is no perfect way to eat a meal.* There are many more meals at which you can make adjustments. That's why acceptance is a very important cornerstone of *Simply Mindful Meal by Meal.* Mindful acceptance of your previous meal—regardless of the level of your mindfulness or how much you ate—is vital.

By accepting your meal and the choices you make today, you are being kind and compassionate toward yourself.

May I remind you of one more thing. *You* are the one taking this journey, so please tailor *Simply Mindful Meal by Meal* in a way that works best for you! If you have something in particular that you would like to work on, by all means use the mindful eating meditations that apply—even if they are mostly in one section. You could also cycle through the sections, such as using a Step 1 practice for one meal, a Step 2 practice for the next meal, a Step 3 practice for the meal after that, and so on. Another idea is to scan through the pages or Table of Contents and see which topic or meditation "speaks" to you right now. Or, you could decide to open the book randomly and let the Universe be your guide.

However you choose to navigate *Simply Mindful Meal by Meal*, my deepest hope is that these pages season all your days with life-affirming joy, compassion, moderation, acceptance, peace and mindfulness.

* Dear Reader, let me share a final, separate note. Since this is the age where computer simulated writing and language are being

utilized, I feel it's important for you to know that this work is what I am referring to as *Certified HI2*—a term I coined to denote that *Simply Mindful Meal by Meal* has been completely written using *Human Insight and Human Intelligence*. While a machine might be able to sort through data and large language models to provide information about mindful eating, a computer software program, no matter how facile, can never understand true hunger, appetite, craving, emotions, and the whole host of factors that affect eating and body image. Food is a blessing from the natural world from which we cannot be separated, and I hope these pages connect you more deeply with your humanity and the living Earth from which all life springs.

STEP 1

ENTRY, HUNGER AND CHOICES

The 4-Step Food Journey starts with an awareness of how you enter each meal. By noticing your emotions and hunger, you can make new conscious choices that will dramatically enhance your mealtime experience. Invite deeper peace, awareness and acceptance into your life by applying the simple meditations and practices in this section.

1

ENTRY

Be Mindful of Your Emotions

Lead me not into temptation;
I can find the way myself.
—Rita Mae Brown

E ach meal brings emotional challenges. Have you ever eaten a meal while you were angry, frustrated, or upset? Eat a meal in anger and you eat anger. Contemplate this story before today's meal:

Two monks—one young and one elderly—gather food for their daily meal. On their way back to the monastery, a woman falls into the nearby river and struggles against the current. Without hesitation, the eldest monk carries her safely to the shore. The monks continue walking in silence until the young monk can no longer contain his anger.

"You carried that woman and broke your monk's vow that said you are not to touch a woman."

"I left her on the bank," says the old monk. "But I am afraid you are still carrying her on your shoulders."

PRACTICE/MEDITATION

What emotions do you carry with you as you enter a meal? This might be anger, frustration, boredom, or loneliness, etc. Where is the emotion in your body? If you can feel it—such as a sensation of tightness, emptiness, or pain—do the following: Inhale and picture a healing breath traveling to wherever in the body you feel that sensation.

Let the breath dissolve or soften the sensation. Then, as you exhale, imagine the breath carrying the negative emotion or energy down the body and out through the bottom of the feet and back into the Earth. Take as many breaths as you need to let go of that emotion.

Accept that it's okay to feel emotions. But carrying them into your mealtime can bring unintended consequences, from emotional eating to making unhealthy food choices.

Knowing your emotions is a useful mealtime preparation and practice. Routinely bring awareness to your pre-meal emotions, and you'll enjoy eat bite and morsel a little bit more.

2

HUNGER

Is Hunger Physical or Emotional?

Every new cycle of growth, every step we take toward
a deeper realization of self, every death and rebirth
of our current and future identity adds a wonderful sheen
to our veneer, to our character . . . to our crust.
—Brother Peter Reinhart

What is the "crust" or emotional energy you bring with you to today's meal? Are you excited to gain sustenance and meaning? Or are you tired and worn out, just going through the motions of eating?

It helps to understand where you are in your own personal cycle of growth. You, like all of nature, possess a season, a time for growth and expending energy, or a time for slowing down and repose. There is a time for nourishing the body and a time for letting go of hunger. If you have been pushing your body and mind hard while at work, for example, consider how that will affect your food choices and experience.

Does your body need more food, or less? What does your hunger tell you about the *kind* of food your body truly wants at this moment? Is your hunger physical or emotional? The answers to these questions can be found by turning your attention inward and listening deeply.

PRACTICE/MEDITATION

When talking about hunger here, we are referring to physical hunger. Often, though, hunger is driven by negative emotions that can cause anyone to seek out food in order to feel comfort or distract from negative feelings.

To find the root of your hunger, begin by taking a few long, slow breaths. Breathing out, know you are breathing out. Breathing in, know you are breathing in. How wonderful!

Next, tune into your body. Emotions are held in the body, so feel where you feel tight, tense, upset or constricted. Is there a name you can give to what you are feeling? If you're not sure, that's okay. It can take time to know and label your emotions.

For instance, if you are feeling lonely, sad, hurt or angry, then you may be experiencing emotional hunger. And while food may offer some temporary relief or distraction, it will not make emotional pain or discomfort go away for very long.

Just knowing the difference between physical and emotional hunger is a good place to start. If you experience physical hunger, then eat. If you experience emotional hunger, then identify the emotion and name it. Invite the peace that comes from learning the difference between these different kinds of hunger.

3

CHOICES

Make One Small Change Today

Fight your shame.
Throw out your pride
and learn all you can from others.
This is the basis of a successful life.
—16th century tea master Rikyu

Meals represent a series of choices. Each choice is like a step that takes you in a particular direction. Over the years, similar choices, or habits, can lead you very far in one direction.

Ultimately, though, you are always free to choose another direction. You are always free to take a new step that is beyond habitual choice. Remember that healthy eating is also a habit and that change is always possible. What one, small, achievable step can you take today? Even if you choose to eat one bite of a food that you think would be beneficial for you, it is enough for now. What would that food be? What foods not on your current "choice" list could contribute to your well-being? (*If there are medical reasons for food choices, those need to be taken into account.*)

PRACTICE/MEDITATION

For this meditation you will reflect on various questions. Honesty is important here. Blaming and shaming, however, are optional and not recommended! Take a slow breath as you reflect on the following:

Do I tend to eat the same foods day after day?

Are there foods that I fear or are "off limits"?

Is eating more of a worry and a chore than a joy?

What would it be like for me to make one small, new food choice today?

If there is rigidity in your choices or if you feel stuck and conflicted about your choices, this could be a signal for you to be more "flexible." Imagine for a moment, that you have a more "flexible" and open way of making food choices.

Pay attention to people around you who are healthy and active. You might want to experiment by trying some of the foods others find energizing and enjoyable. Don't be afraid to ask others about food choices. Keep in mind that we are not talking about "diets" because those tend to reduce choice or limit choice. Moderation is the key.

4

ENTRY

Naming Mealtime Emotions

Waiting is a state of mind.
Basically, it means that you want the future;
you don't want the present.
—Eckhart Tolle, *The Power of Now*

The subtle feelings you have about your next meal can cause you to feel anxiety, anticipation, excitement, fear, calm, and even peace. As you await your next meal, what is your state of mind? If you are not sure, pause for a moment as you make your way to the next meal. Take a breath and feel any restriction in your breath, body or mind.

Sometimes feelings are subtle, like a gently shifting wind. Let yourself sense the breeze within you. Rest in the knowledge that you don't need to push away any feelings about food or eating. When you push something away, does it not often push back even harder? If you are fearful of eating, for example, let yourself sense your fear.

PRACTICE/MEDITATION

As you prepare for the next meal, what emotions are you bringing along with you? Allow yourself to rest in the body. It can help to take a nice breath or two and ask, "What am I feeling right now?"

If you are new to labeling or naming your emotions, this can take some practice. It might help for you to reflect back on the earlier events of your day. Did you experience stress, frustration, anger, hurt, numbness or any other feeling? If so, are you still carrying that feeling with you into your meal?

Research has shown that high levels of stress can cause emotional eating and a host of unhealthy eating choices. By naming your emotions, you are acknowledging and accepting them instead of being in the grip of them. If there's tension or tightness in the body, that can be a clue that an emotion is related to that sensation. Take a few moments to assess and name your emotion.

Congratulations on pausing to reflect on what you are feeling before you eat. With self-knowledge of emotions, you gain a measure of peace and self-mastery. Simply acknowledge that this is what you feel at this moment. To do this is to live with grace and self-acceptance at a deep level.

5

HUNGER

What Is Your Body Hungry for?

The food is brahma *(creative energy)*
Its essence is vishnu *(preservative energy)*
The eater is shiva *(destructive energy)*
No sickness due to food can come
To one who eats with this knowledge.
—Sanskrit blessing

With each bite, we absorb the energy essence of food. Has food ever made you drowsy, excitable, or calm? In ancient Hindu thought, for example, all physical matter is believed to be formed by the condensed vibratory energy of the cosmos.

This energy—which becomes part of us when we eat—takes three basic forms. The "first energy" is called *tamas*, which has qualities that cause us to become tired, lazy, slow, weak, and dull. The next, *rajas*, possesses qualities that cause increased heat, ambition, hunger, and emotion. The remaining energy, *sattva*, fills us with balance, harmony, composure, and spiritual lightness.

PRACTICE/MEDITATION

As you prepare for the next meal, what would it be like for you to tune into the kind of energy your body is hungry for and could use right now?

First, find a quiet place where you can either journal or reflect for a few minutes or moments. As always, it can help to get centered by taking a couple calming breaths or coming into the presence of your body, such as by noticing your feet on the floor and being aware of your posture.

Now, reflect on what kind of energy your body could use right now. It might help for you to recall how certain foods affect your energy level. Which ones cause you to lose energy, feel groggy and hinder your progress? Which ones leave you feeling stimulated, refreshed, light and energetic? Also, ponder those that generate a feeling of well-being and harmony.

Decide which kind of energy your body is hungry for right now. As you prepare your meal or decide what to eat, let your intuition and knowledge of past foods guide you. Like the old adage says: "You are what you eat."

6

CHOICES

Inventory of Your Food Choices

As a child my family's menu consisted
of two choices: take it, or leave it.
—Buddy Hackett

Many times, memories of childhood foods can stay with you—and even subconsciously affect your food choices. Do you remember the foods you ate when growing up? The ones you liked and the ones you hated? These memories may cause you to gravitate towards certain foods that bring a sense of familiarity and comfort, as well as to avoid others.

That is why it is helpful to think about how food choices change over time. Just as we mature and grow from a child into an adult, our food choices need to grow and mature.

PRACTICE/MEDITATION

For this practice, you are going to take a trip down memory lane to explore your food habits over your lifetime. To do this, you will create a "food inventory" and explore how you have the freedom to change your eating habits.

Find a quiet place where you can reflect and jot down the primary foods you ate 1) a child, 2) a teenager, 3) a young adult, and finally now, 4) as an adult. If you are unable to journal, you can just mentally recall the foods you ate. As you do this, put a plus sign (+) by the foods you liked and a minus sign (-) by the foods you didn't like or avoided.

When you are done, take a look at the different categories. What changes do you notice over these four stages? What foods are different? What foods remain the same? Do the food choices increase or decrease over time? Look at the overall pattern. Simply observe the clues as a detective might, or as I like to say, "no blame, no shame." By making this inventory, you are also increasing your food awareness and giving yourself the freedom to make new and more informed choices at the next meal.

7

ENTRY

How Much Will Satisfy Today's Hunger?

You have reproved me for eating very little,
but I only eat to live, whereas you live to eat.
—Socrates

How do you think your diet affects your overall health and longevity? In the 21st century, we pride ourselves on our ever-increasing life expectancy. But many of us may be surprised to learn that the Buddha lived until age eighty, when he died of food poisoning from tainted boar's flesh. Socrates also lived until eighty, when his life prematurely ended because he was forced to drink hemlock. Aristotle and Plato lived to ninety years of age!

How did people who lived more than 2,000 years ago—with no antibiotics—maintain active lives for so long? Given modern medicine, our present-day life expectancy should be 150 years or more. Many ancient Greeks subsisted on a modest diet of unfired vegetables. This confirms what many wisdom traditions tell us: seasonal and local foods may be the most harmonious for our bodies. And, Socrates' practice of moderation in eating seems to have contributed to his long life.

PRACTICE/MEDITATION

Do you live to eat or eat to live? With moderation we can do a little of both. But it's important to tune into your body's signals for what it really needs in the long term, rather than the more temporary craving or desire for a particular taste or feeling. It can help to get in the habit of sitting in silence for at least a minute before eating as a way to discern your hunger.

Most "accidental" or unhealthy eating happens because we aren't aware of moderate hunger levels. Imagine hunger being on a 1-10 scale, where number one represents the absence of hunger and ten is extreme hunger. If you eat when your hunger is in the more extreme 7-10 range, you'll be prone to making choices that are more impulsive. But if you eat when your hunger is in the moderate 4-5-6 range, you'll likely make better choices without eating more than you need.

Rate your hunger level today as you enter your meals. Get to know what different body signals are telling you—whether it's a pang in the gut, a bad headache, or just a subtle sense of wanting to eat. In particular, get to know what your body's moderate hunger signals feel like when in the 4-5-6 range.

Once you're learned to recognize the moderate hunger signals, you can enter your next meal with the question: *What foods, textures, tastes and quantity will best satisfy this hunger right now?*

8

HUNGER

Recognize Impatience and Eat with Calm

Patience takes courage.
—Pema Chödrön, *Comfortable With Uncertainty*

To enter a meal with patience and peace is a way of being gentle and kind. It is a way of recognizing and responding to your own hunger and self-care. How patient are you as you enter mealtime? Does impatience get in the way of answering your hunger? Are you patient towards your hunger?

Patience is not easily understood in our culture. If anything, our lifestyle is greatly measured by speed. Think about it: We drive on expressways. We even check out our food in "express lanes." Microwave meals are ready in minutes, and some takeout restaurants promise 30-minute delivery "to your door or your money back." It's all about getting to the next thing and the next. Cultivating patience and slowing down are important ways to recognize and respond appropriately to the body's hunger signals. When all is said and done, what good are those minutes "saved" in the food checkout express lane if you feel uptight, nervous, and unable to truly nourish yourself?

PRACTICE/MEDITATION

Whatever impatience you have around this next meal, take a deep breath and release it with a slow and satisfying "Aahhhhh." Let your impatience or desire to move on to the next thing dissolve and disperse like a teaspoon of salt in a serene pond.

Dedicate this meal to eating each bite in peace. Take a conscious breath before each bite. Chew slowly. Taste the food. When you are ready, swallow intentionally. Yes, there is just this bite . . . just this everlasting, intimate moment of awareness. Each time you notice your desire or thought to move on to the next thing, take another breath.

Feel your body in the chair. Notice the colors of the food on your place. Recall the history of your food, how it was originally planted, watered, nurtured, harvested and made available for you. How miraculous!

As you eat, take a moment to notice your level of hunger. Is it less than when you began eating? By eating slowly, you give your body enough time for it to send satiety signals letting you know you've eaten enough to nourish you. Eating too quickly, it's easy to eat too much before you get the signal that you're full and no longer hungry.

Don't put a time limit on your meal. Give yourself permission to eat in peace. This is a form of Grace that you give to yourself. Amen.

9

CHOICES

Kitchen Mindfulness

Your karma is in the refrigerator.
—Donald Altman

D o you often go to the refrigerator or the convenience store without really knowing what you want to eat? You can practice "refrigerator mindfulness" by taking stock of how your shopping choices create your future karma around food.

For example, if your refrigerator and pantry are only stocked up with ice cream, cookies and other sugary foods, that's probably what you'll end up eating when you're hungry.

How can you broaden your choices so that you can cultivate a taste for various flavors and textures, including fresh and unprocessed foods?

§

PRACTICE/MEDITATION

What's in your refrigerator at this moment? What foods populate your pantry?

For this meditation, you will simply observe, like a neutral witness, the food choices that you have available at home. Imagine, for a moment, that you are a detective who has never been in this kitchen before. By investigating the foods you find, what clues might this give you about the health and emotional state of the person who bought them?

Remember, you are not being judgmental as you do your food inventory. You are just being curious and observant like a detective! When you have completed your kitchen mindfulness observations, sit and reflect on what you've learned. You could journal your observations as well. What changes in food choices would you recommend? How would other kinds of food choices produce a healthier and more satisfying kitchen karma?

10

ENTRY

Letting Go of Mealtime Expectations

Not-knowing can be the doorway to true knowing
—Sanaya Roman, *Spiritual Growth*

When you enter a restaurant or eat at home, do you have a set idea of how it will turn out? Do you believe that the experience will be pleasant? Are you determined to stick to a pre-arranged eating plan?

But no matter how hard we may try to control mealtime, the unexpected frequently happens. When a menu change or a food temptation derails your best-laid plans, how do you feel afterwards?

In one sense, the idea of "not-knowing" can be about releasing our expectations. The Buddha made the point that if we accept what is already present in our life then we will not be disappointed. Yet the moment we set ourselves up with expectations, we also set ourselves up for unhappiness and dissatisfaction.

Not having expectations does not mean that you have no goals, no hopes, no desires for your next meal. But it does mean that you loosen your grip, ever so slightly, on the outcome.

PRACTICE/MEDITATION

As you prepare to enter this next meal, what are your expectations? Maybe that's a question you've never even asked yourself before. If so, take a moment to reflect on those meals where you wished you had done something differently, such as having eaten less, changed your food selection, eaten at a different time or place, or even sat somewhere else.

Dissatisfaction often comes from our resistance to experiencing things just as they are. So, consider how you might feel if you did not resist this upcoming meal. That means, accepting whatever happens at mealtime, whether it's in or out of your control. Yes, you will still make decisions, but you can accept the outcome no matter what.

Before entering your meal, you might even sit with the words, "May I accept this meal as the gift that it is." You could also picture yourself eating in peace, with full acceptance of whatever the meal may bring.

Sit for at least a minute or two until you feel at peace with this openness toward the uncertainty that awaits you. By doing this, you are also releasing expectations and being present with the journey of your next meal. How wonderful!

11

HUNGER

Make Friends with Hunger

Sitting quietly, doing nothing,
Spring comes,
and the grass grows, by itself.
—Matsuo Bashō, Japanese Poet

If you do not sense hunger but find you eat anyway, it might help to follow nature's example. Grass grows when Springtime comes. Rain clouds rain without wondering whether they will ruin someone's picnic. Each flower, each blade of grass, moves to the ticking and beat of its own time clock.

Humans also have natural rhythms. Let your rhythms guide you and help you more naturally discover when you are hungry—not emotionally hungry, but *physically* hungry. The number of meals eaten daily varies from culture to culture. Our society tells us three meals a day at set times are the norm. But what is really best for you? When does your hunger blossom?

Generally, though, do not skip breakfast. Sometimes, not eating can make weight loss more difficult because the body slows your metabolism to conserve energy. A hearty early meal signals your body's metabolism that you are active. It can help to include protein, which activates the executive and decision-making areas of the brain.

PRACTICE/MEDITATION

For this meditation you will make friends with your hunger. Remember that physical hunger is an ancient signal that prompts you to seek out that next meal.

Reflect back for a moment. How do you normally heed your hunger signals? Do you wait until they get intense before springing into action? Do you have a backup plan for answering hunger if you are busy and no food is available?

Right now, sit and let yourself explore and examine your hunger. To begin, feel your body as you breathe. Notice your feet on the floor. Next, notice when your hunger starts to blossom. What does it feel like? Where do you notice it in the body? If hunger was a friend inviting you to eat, what might it say?

By answering your hunger, you are connecting with yourself in the present moment. You can even ask the hunger, "What would you like to eat right now? What are you desiring that will help provide the body with long lasting, healthy energy?"

In addition, you could create a back-up plan for bringing snacks with you for those times when you might need them. To do this makes hunger a friend, as well as demonstrates self-care and self-kindness.

12

CHOICES

Expanding Food Preferences

The path is easy
For those who have no preferences.
—Sanaya Roman, *Spiritual Growth*

Have your food selections ever caused you emotional pain and suffering? This could have something to do with how strongly attached you are to your choices. There is a big difference, for example, between obsessions and preferences.

Obsessions are very strong, singular desires, ideas, or beliefs that have become inflexible and rigid—even if they can cause you harm. I know of a woman who had only chocolate bars in her refrigerator. She offered many reasons why this made sense, but actually, she wanted a better way to feed her hunger with a healthy balance of nutrients. Does that mean that passionately loving chocolate bars is bad? Not necessarily—if they are a preference.

That's because preferences allow us to go beyond all-or-none thinking. They represent a choice that allows for flexibility, adaptation and change. So if chocolate is not available, then maybe a piece of fruit will do. By contrast, a singular, or obsessive, point of view—about vegetables, chocolate, or any idea—blocks out your choices and limits your freedom.

PRACTICE/MEDITATION

For this practice, you will reflect on being flexible and less restrictive with food choices. To begin, think about the foods that are in your "absolutely love" list—those foods or food groups that you tend to eat most frequently (or even exclusively). Now, reflect on your "absolutely hate" list—foods that for whatever reason, you avoid like the plague.

Spend a few moments, or minutes, reflecting on when these lists formed. How old were you? What was happening in your life at that time you put foods into a particular category?

Now, ask yourself: *How willing are you to depart from these limited, all or none lists?* Take some calming breaths as you consider expanding your food choices. To begin, imagine changing the "totally love" list into a new category called, "preferred foods." In other words, these are foods you like but are not rigidly attached to them. They are simply preferred.

At the same time, try to imagine moving those "absolutely hate" foods into a category called, "possible foods." You may not eat these possible items very often, but they are no longer rigidly avoided or excluded from your diet.

Throughout the day, notice which categories you typically put foods into. Then, consciously move them into a new, more expansive and less restrictive category. Now, congratulate yourself on bringing greater courage and openness to your food choices.

13

ENTRY

The Most Best Place to Start Healing

You might be the most depressed person in the world,
the most addicted person in the world,
the most jealous person in the world . . .
All of that is a good place to start.
—Pema Chödrön, *Start Where You Are*

What is your most difficult eating issue? Do you eat too much? Do you eat less than is good for you? Are you rigid with your choices? Are you addicted to potato chips, ice cream, or any food? Do you emotionally beat yourself up for eating the things you think you "shouldn't?" Think of your worst food problem, and you have just found the best place for you to start.

Thinking about where you "should" be often creates an obstacle. This "should" thought gets you (and many of us) into trouble, because it focuses on guilt and blame rather than accepting the joyful truth of your starting place. Only by being mindful of your emotional hunger can you truly deal any issue or the pain surrounding it.

PRACTICE/MEDITATION

What can you acknowledge about your emotions around food, body and eating? This is not a blaming or judging form of honesty, but rather, an honest awareness of what is occurring in this moment. Wherever you are right now is the best place for you to begin.

Today's practice asks you to think of your inner emotions and negative thoughts as mental "selfies" or "posts" that you put online. Instead of responding to your inner posts, just let yourself get curious. By stepping back and simply observing them in this more open and neutral way, you can watch all your thoughts from a safe distance. This shift of awareness frees you from mental reactivity and allows you to simply watch and notice your mental posts without grabbing onto them or letting them provoke you!

Just as importantly, it lets you find compassion and kindness, especially during those times when you might be having emotionally difficult or self-judging thoughts. Simply notice how your mind works, without grabbing onto old, repetitive thought habits that say very little about who you really are.

When you notice blaming or shaming thoughts or feelings around your food habits, take a gentle, calming breath. Breathe in peace and compassion. Find spaciousness here, in this moment, for yourself as you learn to notice your inner mental activity and realize that it does not define you.

And, each time you notice one of those old, automatic mental posts, you can smile and say, "Aha, I caught you!"

14

HUNGER

Forgiveness of Food Choices

For months the fool may fast,
eating from the tip of a grass blade.
Still he is not worth a penny
beside the master whose
food is the way.
—The Buddha, *Dhammapada*

Have you ever struggled with controlling your food choices and/or the quantity of food you eat? If so, then you are in good company. That is because Buddha, Jesus, and others learned that food moderation was vital to health and spiritual growth. Jesus revolted against the strict food laws of his time by saying, "there is nothing outside a man which by going into him can defile him; but the things which come out of a man are what defile him." Then there was the Buddha, who gave up fasting for the "middle way" of eating in moderation—and shortly after attained enlightenment.

You may be doing yourself a disservice by defining yourself so narrowly by what you eat—thereby creating separations between yourself and others, when compassion would be the wiser course.

PRACTICE/MEDITATION

How strongly do you identify with your food choices? Sometimes, food choices are put into categories of "right" or "wrong." For example, dictating the kind of foods that others should eat—such as for weight, health or moral reasons—probably indicates a strong identification with various choices.

Right now, take some calming breaths. When you are settled in, rate your identification with the foods you eat on a 1-10 scale, with 1 being a very low identification to 10 representing a very strong identification.

What would it be like for you to soften your identification with your food choices? Do your choices make you feel righteous? Smarter? Safer? More enlightened? For a moment, reflect on the following question: Who would you rather have as a neighbor, a kind meat eater or a cruel vegetarian? A forgiving junk food eater or a strict and judgmental health addict?

When we take extreme positions, we may lose the tender parts of ourselves and create barriers with others. Sit in silence and soften as you offer a dollop of tolerance and forgiveness for yourself and others. Doing this can also allow you to follow your hunger to more diverse items on your daily menu.

15

CHOICES

Add Well-being Foods to Your Diet

It's an angry fish because it swims against the tide.
If I'm feeling lethargic I eat salmon.
—Boy George, pop singer

When you are feeling sick or weak, what foods do you instinctively seek out? Do you eat a simpler, more pure and wholesome diet? Do you eat less, giving your body a rest from heavy digestion? (While you are at it, make sure you are getting enough sleep.)

Many traditions accept the idea that you take on the energy characteristics of the food you eat. Traditional Chinese medicine practitioners, for example, place great emphasis on the purity and energy of a food. Some foods are believed build up and sustain your *ch'i*, or body's energy. Foods with little nutritional value, such as junk food filled with high levels of sugar and refined starches, do not increase your storehouse of *ch'i*. Worse, they may weaken it, thus making you susceptible to disease and exhaustion.

PRACTICE/MEDITATION

For the practice, you will reflect on how foods make you feel after you've consumed them. Does sugary food give you quick energy, but cause you to crash after a short while? Which foods give you longer, sustaining energy? Which make you feel lighter, happier, or refreshed? Which make you feel lethargic, slow, or sleepy? Food combinations make a difference too. To begin, create a Food Journal with three columns on a sheet of paper.

- Above the left hand column write "Foods/Meals." Here you will track the foods and quantities you ate at your meal.
- In the center column write "Energy." For this column, include both how your body and mind felt—such as slow, energized, sleepy, buzzed, crashed, full, relaxed, fidgety, refreshed, light, creative, sluggish, etc. Be sure to note how long different energies lasted or how they changed over time.
- In the right hand column, write "Emotions/Feelings." In this column, make sure to write all the different emotions that were elicited from your foods. This could be anything including happy, elated, bright, calm, dull, sad, angry, anxious, frustrated, irritated, annoyed, thoughtful, patient, uneasy, impatient, curious and others.

After a month, review your Food Journal and look for trends and similarities. You will likely identify foods you'll want to avoid and others that you'll want to include more often in your daily diet.

16

ENTRY

Centering with a Mindful Moment

Man shall not live by bread alone,
but by every word that proceeds from the mouth of God.
—Jesus, *Matthew 4:4*

One good way to become centered before stepping onto mealtime's center stage is to recall your deep spiritual connection. This is true in many of the world's wisdom traditions. How did Jesus, for example, maintain the strength to survive in the wilderness for forty days and nights without food? Likewise, the Prophet Muhammad received many revelations during periods of fasting. Clearly, spiritual strength can be gained by focusing on prayer and the word of God/Goddess or the Divine.

Spiritual energy, for example, is a necessary component of fasting. It can also help you overcome other difficult obstacles and challenges. Spiritual focus requires energy and discipline, and is like any skill. That is why, in order for you to succeed with any healthy eating plan, you need to engage skillpower, not willpower.

PRACTICE/MEDITATION

For this practice, you will use a word, phrase or image that you can focus your attention on as you enter your mealtime. You could think of this as a mealtime entry mantra that brings you into alignment with your deeper aspirations for this upcoming meal.

If you already have a spiritual practice, you might have a prayer or spiritual word that you find centering and helpful. If not, think of a word or phrase, or even an image, that conveys what you want to invite into your daily meal. This might be a sense of discipline, love, peace, acceptance, calm, balance, or patience, to name a few. Once you pick an image, word, phrase or prayer that feels right, you can focus on before mealtime.

In fact, any of the words mentioned above could work perfectly. What's important is that your chosen word/s resonate with you and what you would like to manifest at your next meal, as well as in your life.

Find a quiet place, ideally with a view to nature, where you can sit with your word/image/prayer, etc., for about five minutes. To begin, set your intention for how your prayer or word or image can enhance your upcoming meal.

Then, bring awareness to your word/image/prayer without forcing it. If you get distracted, that okay—and quite normal. So just recognize that you are distracted and gently return your focus and attention back to the mealtime entry mantra. If you want to do this longer than five minutes, that's okay too. As you enter your mealtime space, feel how your word/prayer/image is still with you.

17

HUNGER

Experience the Body's Seasonal Needs

Feed the sacred flame with healthy food,
at proper intervals . . . for the maintenance
of a robust and healthy body.
—Gopi Krishna, *Kundalini*

Does your hunger align with the season of the year? For example, how has your winter diet prepared you for the coming of spring? If you live in a snowy winter climate, do you eat a lot of warm, heavier dishes that fortify you against the cold? Or, if you live in a warmer locale, how does your eating change with the seasons?

Is your eating in tune with each season? For example, Spring's approach is made evident by the lengthening of the days. The rains of March and April prepare the ground for planting. The trees awaken with buds. Do you feel yourself awakening to the call of lighter, cooler, fruits and vegetables? Are you feeling more energetic as the days lengthen?

How does your hunger change when the days shorten with the coming of the fall and winter seasons?

ॐ

PRACTICE/MEDITATION

For this meditation, you will recall how your hunger is affected by the seasons. Whatever time of year it is right now, reflect on how your dietary and energy needs change season-by-season. Do you tend to crave different food types, textures, or temperatures at various times of the year?

You can also ask yourself: How have different seasonal foods helped you to cope better with stress. What foods are grown in your regional area? You might want to try these, even if you never have, as a way to align with the climate and season where you reside. Allow yourself to adapt and be flexible with the seasons, just as all plants and nature dance in harmony with mother Earth.

18

CHOICES

Personal and Planetary Well-being

Whenever I make a choice, I will ask myself two questions:
"What are the consequences of this choice that I am making?"
and "Will this choice bring fulfillment and happiness to me
and also to those who are affected by this choice?"
—Deepak Chopra

When you hear the word ecosystem, what do you think about? Actually, there are many different ecosystems. Your body, for instance, is a self-contained, incredibly efficient ecosystem. Your lungs are like the air, your blood like the rivers and streams. What foods best help to maintain your personal ecosystem in balance and harmony?

Bear in mind that the choices you make for your personal ecosystem also have an impact on world's ecosystem. What is the impact on the planet of raising cattle or growing genetically modified cereals and grains? There are many books written on these topics, such as Francis Moore Lappé's *Diet for a Small Planet.*

I do not mean, for example, that you should stop eating beef or other foods that sustain you. However, it benefits you to become more aware of your food choices—for yourself, your children, and all beings.

PRACTICE/MEDITATION

Get settled in as you bring your focus to the breath. With each in-breath, notice how your body absorbs the outer world into its ecosystem. With each out-breath, notice how you release part of your inner world to intermingle with the larger ecosystem.

The air from each breath taken by every living being, even those breaths taken by long deceased ancestors, is still circulating among us. Plants, too, take in and release molecules that intermingle with the entire ecosystem.

Spend the next few minutes being aware of the intermingling of the outer and inner ecosystems. These are in contact always. The separation you feel with the outer world is more tenuous and precarious than you might think. Simply let yourself feel the inner-outer connection as you continue to breathe.

As you complete this meditation, you might reflect on how your dietary needs affect others with whom you co-share and co-inhabit the larger ecosystem. How beautiful!

19

ENTRY

Wondrous Possibilities

Knowledge of what is possible is the beginning of happiness.
—George Santayana, philosopher

Suppose you knew that your next meal would be the most amazing and profound experience of your life? How would that change your next meal? Frankly, you would probably run there as fast as you could.

As strange as it may sound, your next meal *can* be the beginning of joyfulness. It can be the dawn of greater awareness of your food habits. It can be the awakening of a food memory. It can be the first time you make a new food choice. It can present a new way of communing with the divine. It can be a window into making a deeper connection with someone. It can even offer you a mindful taste and a new flavor of food.

All this, and more, is possible. It is all waiting for you . . . at your next meal.

PRACTICE/MEDITATION

As you prepare to eat your next meal, spend some time reflecting on the multitude of possibilities before you. For example, there's the awareness that each bite you take is unique and different from the one that came before. You can notice the complex web of connection and preparation that brings food to your plate, from the cultivation and harvesting to the processing and shipping. Allow yourself to open to the possibilities of a new food choice, a new flavor, a new texture, and new awareness about the food on your plate.

Can you imagine the sunlight, air, nutrients from the soil, and rain clouds that helped your food grow and flourish? All of these are contained in each bite that you take.

And then, let's remember that there's the possibility of intimacy and connection that comes when sharing food with friends, family and others. And, who knows? This next meal may even open you up to the possibility of kindness by offering food to others.

As you sit down for your next meal, remember to invite these and other wonderful possibilities to the table.

20

HUNGER

The Liberating Power of Moderation

Man does not live by bread alone.
Every now and then he needs a cookie.
—Groucho Marx

I f you take your food journey too seriously, then you will miss out on all the fun and enjoyment and nurturing that food offers you. Moderation means that you allow yourself the freedom to break free of rigid and constricting boundaries and definitions.

When you rigidly set unreasonable standards—zero sugar, zero carbs, or zero "fill in the blank"—then who are you punishing and why? Freedom to choose is not indiscriminate. It comes with the responsibility to choose wisely.

Let me share a story of when I was having lunch with the monks in the monastery. I had noticed that the abbot and well-known mindfulness teacher U Silananda normally avoided sweets. But one day, when a young ten year old girl offered him a sweet pastry during lunch, he bowed his head, thanked her and graciously ate it. Later, when I asked him about this, he said that while he didn't really like sweets, he had eaten the pastry out of kindness for the girl who offered it as a gift. To not do so would have been ungracious.

PRACTICE/MEDITATION

Dieting is often about controlling our desires and hunger by defining which foods to eat, and which ones to avoid. But the reasons diets often fail is that they are too rigid. What's needed is moderation.

For this meditation, you will reflect on the "rules" you have about food. How rigid are these rules? Also, what happens when you break them? Do you feel a sense of guilt and shame?

You may even think back to earlier in your life and the lessons you learned about food and eating. Make sure you take some calming breaths before you start. As you reflect, you can also ask, "What if these rules didn't exist?" Yes, rules can serve a purpose as a guideline, but if they are too strict or rigid they can also cause harm.

When you are ready, reflect on the idea of moderation with food and what that would look like for you. One definition for moderation is "to do what is neither extreme nor harmful to oneself or others." It can also mean to do what is moderate and kind to yourself or others.

And so, while savoring a cookie might break a "no sugar rule," at the same time the action is not really harmful. In fact, it may bring joy.

21

CHOICES

What Messages Do Your Food Choices Send?

All things are connected . . .
Man did not weave the web of life;
he is merely a strand in it.
Whatever he does to the web, he does to himself.
—Ted Perry, author

Every day, decisions are made about which food products are put on grocery store shelves. Companies sometimes pay to have their cereals or other products positioned favorably on the shelf.

When it comes to having a say in such matters, it sometimes seems like we are too small, too insignificant to have our voices really heard. But is this really so? Communal actions have created laws requiring nutritional information on food products. In addition, you make your voice heard each time you make a purchase. That's because if no one buys a particular product, it will soon be replaced with another. By learning which foods are good and which are suspect, your choices can create positive change.

PRACTICE/MEDITATION

This movement meditation is best done while shopping at your favorite grocery market. You might think of this as an exercise in conscious or intentional shopping.

Take a few centering breaths before you enter the market. If you are pushing a cart or holding a bag, bring awareness to your hands and how they hold onto the cart or bag. Broaden your awareness to take in the totality of the store. Notice all the colors, the sounds, the music, the scents and the people. It's quite overwhelming, actually! Keep in mind that there's a lot of retail research conducted so that you will buy more and stay longer in the grocery store.

Move slowly, with awareness. Observe the route by which you move through the store. Is this your typical, predetermined route or are you freely moving about moment-by-moment? Neither choice is right or wrong. Just bring awareness to what you are doing.

As you move about, notice your food choices. What draws your attention? Are there sections you are drawn to? Where in the store are those foods that are more highly processed? Where are the less processed foods? It's good to be aware of this, regardless of your choices.

Finally, reflect on how your choices could be impacting the web of life. When leaving the store, you might give thanks or say a blessing for having so many choices and so much to be grateful for.

22

ENTRY

Honoring Today's Meal

The Sabbath is a bride,
and its celebration is like a wedding.
—Abraham Joshua Heschel, *The Sabbath*

Do you celebrate your every meal? Do you ever imagine that you *could?* Well, you can. Just use your entry time to explore your options and get a sense of the joy that your next meal offers.

How about: Eating at an outdoor café or park? Laughing and sharing stories with friends and associates? Sitting in sublime, quiet solitude. Eating while reading a favorite book or tuning into a favorite podcast.

Use your entry moment to tap into and express your creativity. Making each meal a celebration means that you honor that meal, just like you honor someone's birthday, graduation, or anniversary. Put a new celebratory spin on your eating and let go of the burden.

By adding new meaning to your meal or diet, you are also honoring yourself and creating a new relationship to food.

ぷ

PRACTICE/MEDITATION

Today's meditation is about celebrating that next meal and finding a way to make it special. To begin this process, get centered with the breath. Find a location where you can sit without interruption.

One good place to start your reflection is to inquire, "What makes my meals mundane or ordinary?" Repetition or an old mindset are two culprits that can bring boredom into mealtime. Or, maybe you consider a meal as something to get out of the way so you can get on to more important things?

Yes, you may have some very good reasons for speeding through mealtime. But you can elevate even a time-limited or mundane meal into something more meaningful. Next, reflect on how you could make your next meal "celebration worthy!" Here are a few ideas:

1) Honor someone at the next meal, such as having lunch in honor of a parent, a loved one, or a pet. Spend a few moments thinking about them before and during your meal.

2) Give your meal a celebratory name or theme. Any idea works, from "First Meal of the Rest of My Life" and "Trying a New Food Meal" to spiritual themes like "Remembering My Blessings" and "Thankful Thursdays."

Above all, have fun and create new ideas that keep you engaged and celebrating all that a meal can be.

23

HUNGER

Awaken to the Roots of Appetite

My doctor told me to stop having intimate dinners for four.
Unless there are three other people.
—Orson Welles

A strong appetite can drive you to distraction. Has your appetite ever caused you to buy more in a grocery store or order more in a restaurant than you (or maybe Orson Welles) could eat at one sitting? If so, welcome to the club.

Having a good appetite is important because it means you feel your body and its needs. Appetite is useful for another reason. It can help you more deeply tune into your hunger.

Have you ever tried to distinguish between three different kinds of appetite? First, there is your hunger that is provoked by sense desire (seeing, tasting, touching, or smelling food). Next, there is appetite that is stimulated by your physical need for energy, nourishment, and your body's rhythmic clock. Lastly, there is craving for food that is provoked by habit or emotional conditioning, such as wanting comfort food when feeling stressed or lonely.

ॐ

PRACTICE/MEDITATION

For this meditation, you will practice identifying the root of your hunger. Remember that there are three kinds of hunger at work here.

The first is hunger that comes from food-related triggers. Have you seen or smelled food recently? Seeing food can stimulate hunger where none might have existed before, such as when pizza or treats are brought into a workplace. Or, you might simply be imagining food in the mind's eye. Any of these triggers can create a desire or craving for food, which is a hunger that you experience in the mind, the nose, and the senses.

Secondly, hunger can be generated directly by your body's need for energy and nourishment. What is your body feeling? The hunger signals you get from this kind of hunger might be felt in the body. These signals are felt in different ways, such as in the stomach and throughout the nervous system. Even sleepiness, exhaustion, headaches or cramps can be symptoms of hunger. Get to know what your physical sensations of hunger mean. And as discussed earlier, don't wait until the hunger symptoms get extreme.

Thirdly, there is emotional and stress-based hunger that often drives habitual and conditioned hunger. Because this is not physical hunger, you are basically eating to make the "bad" emotional feeling go away. By identifying the root of hunger, you can respond to your physical needs, rather than eat mindlessly because of emotions or cravings.

As you learn to identify these three types of hunger, you'll become more skillful at understanding and knowing how to respond to each.

24

CHOICES

Be Mindful of Food Quality

The quality, quantity, method of preparation,
way of consuming, the place, the time, etc.,
all play an important part in the effect
that food has on us.
—Dr. Vinod Verma, *Ayurveda for Life*

Picking the food you like is important. However, there is also the question of quality. Not all food, for example, is as fresh as you might think. Did you know that apples can be stored for months? Or that tomatoes are often picked before they are ripe and then turned the color red by exposing them to nitrogen?

So, how do you know if the food you are eating is really fresh and pure? Some vegetables include the dates when they were harvested. Also, your local produce manager can be a helpful source of information.

PRACTICE/MEDITATION

For this practice, you will consider ways to get the freshest foods possible. Processed foods—from dairy and meat to canned foods and cereals—typically have expiration dates. Get into the practice of looking for dates on packaging to find the freshest products.

Several companies now provide a service by which local fruits and vegetables are delivered directly to your front door. You can also shop at Farmers Markets—which often require vendors to offer food that is locally grown and is fresh from the fields. These are usually people with a passion for quality who care about the food they provide. (To find local markets, use the the National Farmers Markets Directory at: nfmd.org)

In addition, it can be fun learning how to grow fruits and vegetables of your own. Keep in mind that even a modest raised bed or garden can supply copious amounts of food! You may be surprised at the variety of foods you can plant in your climate zone, and these could provide you with enough homemade salads and meals to last an entire summer. Even if you live in an apartment and have a window sill, you can grow fresh peppers in a pot.

While you're at it, remember to learn about the best ways to store your fruits and veggies at home. All in all, finding fresh foods will add up to a surprisingly enjoyable experience at the dining table.

25

ENTRY

Discover Your Meal's Wisdom Message

Ask and it will be given to you;
seek and you will find;
knock and the door will be opened to you.
—Jesus, *Luke 11:9*

Is there a deeper spiritual meaning, wisdom or message you would like to receive at mealtime? By entering into prayer even before eating, you can be more ready to receive the inner nourishment and fulfillment of food, rather than just getting filled up. Jesus' teaching on prayer is not constrained to the blessing portion of your meal. In truth, prayer extends beyond mealtime.

You can get the most out of your meal by centering and becoming mindful in advance. Sometimes, reading something sacred, poetic, or meaningful can help.

PRACTICE/MEDITATION

Do you have a favorite passage from scripture? Maybe you have a favorite poem? The idea for this entry meditation is to spend a few moments reading a short passage (three or four paragraphs) over and over before you eat. You can think of this as a blessing or prayer. Or, you can imagine this as an open reading where you invite your insight and wisdom to reveal the hidden meaning within.

A similar method of reading to gain insight was used by the Desert Monks in the second and third centuries. It was known as *Lectio Divina*, or divine reading. Typically, the monks would read scripture at mealtime, but you can do this practice before or afterwards just as well.

If there are several people at your meal, each one can find something special to read and share. Each person can take a turn reading aloud the section they like. They can read it once or several times. The only guideline here is to not interrupt a reading. Further, do not try to impose any meaning. Just steep yourself in the words for a few minutes and see how it changes your mindfulness as you prepare to eat.

Sit in silence with appreciation for the person reading and the words they chose. See if any deeper meaning appears for you. If so, and if all agree, you can share your experiences. This is a sacred way to enter any meal with meaning, purpose and togetherness.

STEP 2
PREPARATION AND RITUAL

Cleansing and beautifying the kitchen, as well as transforming food from the mundane to the sacred are the benefits of intentionally including the ingredients of preparation and ritual into each meal. Enjoy the transcendent awareness and mindful fulfillment that naturally arise from using these simple practices and meditations.

26

PREPARATION

Be Mindful of the Simplest Tasks

*Regard all utensils and goods of the
monastery as sacred vessels of the altar.*
—Saint Benedict, *The Rule of St. Benedict*

Cleaning the kitchen can be viewed as an onerous chore to be avoided or seen as a sacred act filled with beauty and devotion.

Did you know that according to the Zen tradition, beginner monks are given easier chores while more experienced monks are given the most menial and demanding chores? Perhaps that is because the Zen masters know that it takes a special kind of wisdom (and person) to appreciate and learn from that which is most simple, plain, and unadorned. Watch your thoughts and attitudes as you clean your kitchen or any workspace. Can you let go of them for long enough to be in the moment with your task?

PRACTICE/MEDITATION

Keep in mind that the first act of meal preparation is uncluttering and cleaning. Prepare the counter space and get your cookware ready and clean before cooking. Preparations also include preparing the dining table.

This is a time for uni-tasking, not multi-tasking. When you are working in a kitchen or preparing a meal, turn off the technology. Do whatever you are doing with full intention, presence and awareness.

When sweeping the floor or cleaning a surface, commit yourself completely to that one thing. You might mentally think, "sweeping, sweeping," or "cleaning, cleaning" or "chopping, chopping" as you perform each act in order to stay present and focused.

Feel each small movement of the body as it experiences whatever you are doing.

It's okay and normal to get distracted. But when this happens, you needn't get frustrated. Simply notice the distraction, then each time, gently and kindly bring yourself back to the task at hand. In this way you are training your mind to focus and be in concert with your task. Wonderful!

27
RITUAL

Create a Personalized Ritual

The fruit of silence is prayer,
The fruit of prayer is faith,
The fruit of faith is love and
The fruit of love is silence.
—Mother Teresa

A ritual prayer—before, during, or after a meal—can transform eating and food from the mundane to the sacred. Sometimes, it can be useful to think about your own history of ritual. As a child, did your family have a mealtime ritual? How was it structured? Most importantly, how did you feel about it? Did the process feel forced? Or was it filled with love and acceptance? Or, if you had no ritual, how do you feel about that now?

However you may have experienced it, how you decide to use ritual in the present is up to you. You have the freedom to shape and transform a mealtime ritual that fits your needs and sensibilities. Whether you live by yourself, as a single parent, with a partner, or as part of a larger family unit, meaningful ritual can add richness and togetherness to ordinary meals. It acknowledges the mystery of food, the awesome wonder of how it nourishes and allows you to reach your life dreams and goals.

PRACTICE/MEDITATION

A mealtime ritual can be represented in many ways. It can be a simple moment of silence. It can be a blessing of thanks or gratitude. The Latin word for gratitude, *gratitudo*, means to find what is pleasing at mealtime. In this way, gratitude is connected to the ritual of saying grace.

A ritual can also be lighting a candle, which represents bringing illumination and awareness into your meal. And, since our being here right now depends on so many others, including ancestors and all who made our living space possible, we can remember and thank them—which makes them part of the ritual as well. Basically, a ritual is any intentional act that helps you pause, reflect and emphasize the importance and sacredness of the food you are about to receive.

What ritual would you like to make part of your meal? Journal or visualize the ritual(s) you would like to integrate into your mealtime. This could include the participation of others around the table. Have fun as you add this special ingredient to your life. You can always make adjustments to your rituals until they work best for yourself and others.

28

PREPARATION

Prepare Your Meal with Intention

Intention combined with detachment leads to
life-centered, present-moment awareness.
—Deepak Chopra

C an you imagine sitting down to eat if you had no real thought about what you were hungry for or just ate to cover up an emotion? The result of such mindless eating might mean eating mechanically, out of habit or to fulfill a craving. Food choices might simply be random or harmful. The beneficial aspects of eating related to making conscious and healthy choices would likely be absent.

However, when you are mindfully aware of your hunger, you can act with the intention to eat a nourishing and satisfying meal. In this case, you will be fully engaged and more able to truly savor each food. Likewise, setting intention with preparation brings mindfulness to the forefront.

Mindfulness in preparation means you are putting your attention on what you are about to do—right now in the present moment. You are not thinking about the appointment you just had or about tomorrow's shopping list.

PRACTICE/MEDITATION

For this meditation, we'll work on staying embodied during meal prep. Why is this important? I vividly recall the time I was leading a weekly mindfulness group and one of the meditators came to class with a large bandage covering her thumb. When I asked what happened, she said with more than a tinge of chagrin, "I was making chopping veggies for a mindful salad. But I got distracted . . . and cut my thumb."

Accidents happen when we're unaware, distracted, multi-tasking, or out of the body. Suppose you're making a mindful salad (or any dish). When you're holding a knife, feel it in your hand. Is the handle cool to the touch? Notice the pressure of your fingers as they wrap around the handle. Feel the weight of the utensil. What is it like when you chop or slice a carrot, onion, mushroom or other food? How do your arm and wrist change position with each motion? How does your elbow tense up and loosen? With mindfulness, there's a lot going on because you're paying attention to every little thing.

Bring awareness into the body as you handle every utensil, pot and pan. If you feel impatience or have thoughts, you can simply notice these. Or, you might label or name them as "impatience" or "thinking." Then, just return to each step with body awareness. How sublime!

29

RITUAL

Recall Food Giveaways for Today's Meal

Do not turn away what is given you,
Nor reach out for what is given to others,
Lest you disturb your quietness.
—The Buddha, *Dhammapada*

All that we have in our kitchen—from the food in the refrigerator to the dishes and condiments in the cabinets—has been offered from some worldly source. Have you ever heard of the traditional Native American ritual called the giveaway? This is a vital ritual through which individuals can experience the extent of giving that exists in our lives and our world. The giveaway asks, first and foremost, that we acknowledge that what we have has all been something given to us.

Think about this. Even though we pay for the meal we eat in a restaurant, it still was created for our benefit. The giveaway asks that we gain the maturity to recognize and be grateful for this, then to give something back. Is this the season of your life to return something?

PRACTICE/MEDITATION

During your meal, recall memorable food giveaways—currently or in the past—that have blessed your life. Bear in mind that awareness that life feeds on life. Whether plant or animal, the food you ingest was at one time a living thing that exchanged molecules with the outer environment, and stored energy that your human cells will absorb in order to maintain life. In other words, your survival depends upon the giveaway of other living beings. It's also dependent on the giveaway of light provided by the sun to plants, the giveaway of nutrients of the soil, and the giveaway of rain for the water that makes life possible.

In some cultures, harvesting of plants is done purposefully so that a few of the plants are left behind. Rather than taking everything, how can we give something back without being greedy and taking everything the Earth gives us?

Even leaving something on your plate, or offering part of your food to others, can act as a giveaway. At today's meal, reflect on the giveaway of energy that sustains you. Then, think how you can share the bounty that you have with others.

30

PREPARATION

Rearrange Your Kitchen

*To be blind is bad, but worse it is
to have eyes and not to see.*
—Helen Keller

Close your eyes for a moment. Can you visualize your cooking and preparation space? Whether your kitchen is large, small, or efficiency-sized, try to identify where everything is without looking. Now think about that space in more detail. Is everything you need to prepare a meal easy to find? Are spices and ingredients where you can find them? Or do you have to dig through cabinets looking for each one? Then there is your preparation space. Is it cluttered or open? Inviting or limiting?

Preparation begins with mindfulness of your working space—whether you are a chef building a salad in your kitchen or simply heating leftovers into the microwave. It is easier and more fun to prepare when your space is clean and uncluttered. The result is perhaps fewer spills and accidents, and a tastier meal.

⚘

PRACTICE/MEDITATION

Think about how you would rearrange your kitchen space to make preparation easier and more fun. Here are a few questions to help with the process:

When is the last time you rearranged your kitchen? What is the first thing you notice when you enter your kitchen space? Is anything out of place? What could beautify your kitchen even a little? Where is your kitchen most cluttered? Where is it uncluttered? Do you have enough space to prepare your meals? What colors draw your attention?

A lot of thought goes into designing professional kitchens and restaurants. One thing you can do is to begin noticing the restaurants you frequent. How do the colors and décor make you feel? Believe it or not, some colors are known to have appetite enhancing qualities, such as red, orange and even yellow. Do some spaces make you feel right at home? Are others cold and uninviting?

You don't have to make wholesale changes to your kitchen and dining space. Even one small change can be helpful if it declutters or adds to the ambience.

31

RITUAL

Spice Up Your Meal

In joy or sadness, flowers are our constant friends.
We eat, drink, sing, dance, and flirt with them.
We wed and christen with them.
—Kakuzo Okakura, *The Book of Tea*

Is there something special that accompanies your mealtime? Sometimes the rituals in your life are so ingrained and invisible that you may not even recognize them. Whether you eat by yourself or with others, "invisible" rituals that enrich your mealtime include such things as music, a vase of flowers, even a lit candle.

There are also unspoken mealtime rituals that touch you every day. In many Asian countries, for example, the eldest is served the food before anyone else gets a chance to fill their plate. Even the western practice of waiting for others to be seated and served before eating is a ritual that declares a sense of courtesy, order and meaning.

Rituals offer you a comforting familiarity that helps to feel normal, even when you may be coping with stress or experiencing difficulties. By adding personal ritual to your meal, you imbue it with a richness that fulfills at many levels.

PRACTICE/MEDITATION

Add a new ritual—flowers, music, and grace—to one of your meals. Did you know, for example, that music can help create a pace for eating a meal? Some studies show that we might eat more quickly with fast-paced music, as well as more slowly with calmer and serene music.

Experiment with adding a new ritual to today's meal. Even the act of eating in silence, such as for the first minute or a meal, is a ritual. How might the inclusion of pictures or memorable items enhance this next meal?

Flowers are often used as symbols of the joy and love that lift our spirits. How can you bring flowers into your ritual table setting? Maybe you have a scented candle or delicate candle holder that can bring a dash of elegance to the table.

Dressing up a dining table with an ornate or pretty table cloth brings a visual and tactile ritual into your space. This is an easy way of saying that this meal is unlike an ordinary one. Another ritual is to include a keepsake from a loved one—such as a family heirloom, utensil or platter.

Finally, allow yourself to have fun with what to add, because what matters most is the intent and meaning bestowed by any object.

32

PREPARATION

Open to Uncertainty

Crack the egg of ignorance.
—Nyishöl Khenpo Rinpoche, Tibetan Buddhist

The entire process of cooking and preparation is all about change and transformation. Bread turns into toast. An unadorned head of lettuce, a hardboiled egg, and a tomato become an enticing fresh salad. Butter, wine, and spices transform into an delectable sauce.

How we go about this makes all the difference. For that reason, I say this: We are all eggs waiting to be cracked. That is because each time we prepare food, our thin outer shell is opened to the space of uncertainty.

We know that the results and outcome of placing a frozen dinner in the microwave cannot always be predicted! Nor should they be.

Let the space of preparation open us to unexpected creativity and growth. Accept this uncertainty with compassion.

PRACTICE/MEDITATION

As you prepare for today's meal, you can begin by setting an intention to release all expectation and open yourself to uncertainty. It might help to recall the words of poet and musician Leonard Cohen, who wrote, "There is a crack, a crack in everything. That's how the light gets in."

During preparation, stay connected to the idea of transformation. Notice how every action you take furthers the process of change. Bring your attention to the changing shapes, colors and textures that appear before you.

Each action is here but for a moment. Preparation is a practice of letting go, of releasing each action and moment in order to make space for the next . . . and the next. If you are holding onto something that doesn't go your way during preparation, such as a negative thought or emotion, that might affect how you move forward.

As the chef or cook or meal preparer, you also are being prepared! You might even notice how you and the meal are inseparable for the moments you spend together. The final meal you serve and enjoy is as much a part of you as you are a part of it.

33

RITUAL

Find the Kernel of Honesty

The spiritual journey does not require going anywhere,
Because God is already with us and in us.
—Father Thomas Keating, *Open Mind, Open Heart*

Following the advice of Father Thomas Keating, ritual opens the door to what is already present at mealtime—or anytime. If you want to feel the depth of your experience, you need to be honest and open. For as Shakespeare once wrote, "To thine own self be true."

The key here is to open up to the *potential* of your connection to spirit and others. Before saying your ritual blessing, give yourself permission to feel the divine presence around you—in whatever form it may take.

If you feel frustrated or bored, let that be your experience of the divine at mealtime. If you feel moved or elated, then that can be your experience. Allow yourself the space to feel differently at each meal. Your mealtime ritual journey is a process, not an endpoint.

PRACTICE/MEDITATION

Reflect on your truth toward food and others during a meal. Allow yourself time for this meditation. Get settled in to your chair. Notice your breathing. Is it fast, slow, rhythmic? Get in tune with your body. Notice your feet on the floor and your body in the chair. What is the position of your legs, knees, arms and hands? Are you sitting upright? You might want to have a relaxed but erect posture, just as if you were going to meditate. And since this is an eating meditation, why not?

Allow some moments of silence. Bring awareness to the space around you, including others who may be nearby or eating with you. Finally, bring awareness to the food on your table or eating space. What are you feeling as you do this—a sense of wonder, gratitude, or surprise?

Next, bring awareness to the heart center. If you want, you can place one or both palms gently over your heart. What are you sensing? You might notice anything from a feeling of warmth and intimacy to a protective covering. Remember that there is no right or wrong here. Whatever you feel is its own validation. If you are not sure about a feeling or sensation, that's okay too. Just get curious and stay present with it.

Likewise, what are you feeling in the stomach or gut area? You might notice other areas of the body as well. Whatever you sense is your personal and honest truth with this meal. Knowing this, accept this meal and your connection with it as you eat and receive nourishment.

34

PREPARATION

Take a Mindful Kitchen Walk

*If you simply read the recipes without putting
them into practice, it's like knowing about peppers,
onions, and garlic, but never knowing how they taste.*
—Ronna Kabatznick, Ph.D., *The Zen of Eating*

Do you ever feel nervous or scattered while planning or making a meal? Mindfulness can soothe mealtime emotions. Interestingly, mindful movement refocuses the mind away from thoughts about the past and the future by solidly placing awareness in the here and now.

This was also true when I worked with clients who struggled with anxiety. After guiding them in a walking meditation around my office, I would then ask, "While we were walking, where were your anxious thoughts?" Usually, they were surprised to discover that those thoughts had vacated. Instead, they were fully focused on taking that next step! Mindful walking is vastly different from just plain walking because it is an intentional practice that brings mind and body closely together. For this meditation, you will spend some practice time walking around your kitchen or other living space either prior to preparation or eating.

PRACTICE/MEDITATION

Mindful walking will slow you down, so if you have never done this before, you might want to walk beside a wall in order to brace yourself and maintain balance.

Begin by simply standing in place, breathing slowly. You'll set a simple intention, "to take a step with my right foot." As you set this intention, follow up by stepping with the right foot. Closely observe the movement of your leg as it steps. That means feeling how your leg lifts up, how the knee bends, how the foot raises off the floor, and how the foot touches down and the body's weight shifts over to the right side. There's a lot happening, isn't there?

Next, you make the intention "to take a step with my left foot," and take that step. Over and over, make this intention followed by action and observation. Mindfulness means being aware of everything—even distracting thoughts and mental judgments (this is too slow, boring, fascinating, etc.). If this happens, just return to the next intention and follow up with the action.

Step as quickly or slowly as your intention lets you for 1-3 minutes, or until you feel centered and balanced. Carry that feeling with you into preparation. When I spent time in a monastery, for example, I usually did a twenty-minute walking meditation outside before breakfast.

35

RITUAL

Manifest Blessings into the World

However many holy words you read,
however many you speak,
what good will they do if you
do not act upon them?
—The Buddha

The Buddha could have been invoking the popular slogan "just do it" with his advice. You invite the sacred into your home and your meal by doing more than just reciting the words of grace. The real objective is to make those words real, to transform them into action, and to manifest them in the world.

Suppose that your mealtime grace includes the idea of thankfulness for the food on your plate. You can naturally extend that thankfulness out into the world by inviting that lonely neighbor to your house for dinner. Maybe you could take part in offering food to others. There are many programs for donating or delivering food, such as *Meals-On-Wheels*, that help you share your thankfulness and your bounty. Just one thing, even a little thing, is a great place to start!

PRACTICE/MEDITATION

The question to reflect on for today's practice or meditation is: *What can I do to bring my blessings into the world?*

You can write down your ideas on a blank sheet of paper. You can also sit in meditation with your breath and reflect on this question. While meditating, an idea, an insight, or even an image may come to you. You needn't have any concrete answers right this moment.

What you are doing is opening yourself to be more aware of possibilities that might exist. For instance, you may notice in the coming days or weeks, an opportunity to manifest your blessing or thoughts for the well-being of others.

You can think of nontraditional ideas as well. Developing a garden or community place to grow foods for those in need can bring people together for the common good. Growing foods locally can also have a broader benefit of reducing the need for the commercial shipping and processing of foods. Maybe your blessing is about offering classes to younger people with the purpose of sharing your unique know-how and expertise. All of these are unique giveaways that you can be a part of.

36

PREPARATION

Moment-by-Moment Meal Prep

*The trouble with ordinary reality is that
a lot of it is dull, so we long ago decided
to leave for somewhere better.*
—Charles Tart, *Living the Mindful Life*

D o you often check out during kitchen preparation and cleaning? Is your mind miles away on a fantasy trip to Hawaii or elsewhere? The psychoanalyst Fritz Perls, who developed Gestalt Therapy, understood this when he said, "Boredom is simply lack of attention."

Really, it is not that ordinary reality is so dull. We just do not pay enough attention to it to see how impressive and fresh it can really be! This sentiment is echoed in an ancient Zen phrase: "Chop wood; carry water." In other words, the real action is right here, in front of us, even in what seems to be the most mundane of actions.

Mindfulness harnesses the power of intention by keeping the mind engaged in the here and now. In an earlier practice (#34) you learned mindful walking. Now, we'll extend that idea into your preparation.

PRACTICE/MEDITATION

Stay mindful during meal preparation is no easy task. There may be kids you are watching, texts you need to answer, pets who are yowling, and a whole host of things and people requiring your attention. The important thing here is not to get too rigid and refuse to attend to others who might need you! Mindfulness also means we can shift gears when necessary. But you can also set the intention to be present with all aspects of preparation, including managing those in your household as well as the meal. Right now, let's focus on meal prep.

While chopping a lettuce, for example, feel the weight of the knife in your hand and the crispness of the produce—all while mindfully following through with the action and observing the results. Each time you arrive at a new step, use another intention, along with observation and action, to enter each fresh moment.

If something urgent calls you away from preparation, you can set the intention to pause or set down your utensils. Continue to set intentions for what you are doing. Stay embodied, as you walk or move about.

You can also set intentions for "setting the table," "placing dishes," "putting food on the plates," and so on. If you forget your intentions or find your mind wandered, just notice where it wandered to and return to engaging your presence. Congratulations on your mindful preparation!

37

RITUAL

Share in Your Ritual Meal

Your spirit is mixing with my spirit
Just as wine is mixing with pure water.
And when something touches You, it touches me.
Now "You" are "me" in everything!
—Al-Hallaj, 10th century mystic and Sufi master

Rituals can sometimes be solemn and serious. But they can just as easily be brimming with a sense of joy, lightness, and laughter. Did you know, for example, that during the Jewish Sabbath, it is considered sinful to worry or be sad? That is why the Sabbath is typically accompanied with song and music. The table setting is beautified with good linen, plates, and utensils. And, the participants dress up in their best clothes.

This makes sense when you realize that the ritual Sabbath represents a shift from the ordinary working week and mundane living into a spiritual dimension. Here, all that matters is the present moment of communion with family and the divine. I know of one family, for example, that created its own ritual meal—complete with candles, singing, a blessing, and beautified table setting. You can do the same.

PRACTICE/MEDITATION

For this practice, you will plan on inviting your family or community to share in creating a special ritual meal. You could make this a weekly gathering or on whatever schedule works best.

Interestingly, research has shown that the family meal is not what it used to be. Because of busyness, overpacked schedules and the ease of popping food in the microwave or grabbing take-out, many family members eat according to their own schedules rather than together at a set time. Nevertheless, it is still possible to create a meal where everyone shares a meaningful time over food.

For your special meal, you might decide to read something special, which is similar to the *Lectio Divina* practice mentioned previously (#25). Or, individuals could share a single thing they are grateful for this day. This gratitude practice can be a powerful experience, as well as being a mindfulness practice because it selectively focuses our attention on something that is pleasant and meaningful.

Family or community members could share input on something to include in the mealtime as a ritual. Either as an object, music, or a blessing. In this way, your special meal illuminates the ideas and feelings of all.

38

PREPARATION

Discover One New Method

Give me the provisions and whole
apparatus of a kitchen, and I would starve.
—Montaigne

Not everyone is at home with a blender or food processor. Whatever your feelings or awkwardness you may feel about more advanced kitchen tools, you can begin simply by working with basic cooking instruments and utensils. Some years ago I attended a professional chef's class. I was very much a novice among a class filled with professionals who ran restaurants and owned catering businesses. That did not stop me from learning.

I remember learning how to roll my French-crafted chef's knife in a graceful up and down motion that quickly diced any vegetable to size. To this day, there is something musical and poetic about the rhythmic sound of the blade tapping on a wooden cutting board. I have kept and cared for that wonderful cutlery.

There is no shame in learning about food, and sometimes the fundamentals are the most fun.

PRACTICE/MEDITATION

Learn a new preparation technique or discover how to use a new utensil or food-related device.

Some of the tricks of the trade that I learned in the chef's class many years ago I still find helpful—whether dicing an onion or slicing an avocado. These methods have also helped me become safer and less prone to injury while handling utensils.

Today, there are many online videos for learning these and other tips recommended by professionals.

For example, do you sharpen your kitchen knives? There are many plug-in devices for doing this, but I still prefer the hand sharpening method, of which there are several types. Choose one new thing you would like to learn about food preparation today. Ideally, it will be something that you can employ as you design today's meal.

39
RITUAL

Invite Stillness as an Honored Guest

True intelligence operates silently.
Stillness is where creativity
and solutions to problems are found.
—Eckhart Tolle, *Stillness Speaks*

I admit it: I am a fast eater. I come from a family of fast eaters that could make a platter of food disappear more quickly than magician David Copperfield. But I'm working on it. Fortunately, the power of mindfulness has helped me discover how ritual brings other dimensions of food to life, such as fulfillment and grace. Even silence.

A mealtime ritual accomplishes four important things. Firstly, it slows you down, giving you a moment of peace by loosening the stimulus-reaction cycle that drives desire and addiction. Secondly, it reconnects you with the divine purpose of food, which is to sustain your body and consciousness. Thirdly, it brings you into communion with the divine, the Earth, and others. Fourthly, it can help establish your food discipline. Even if you say a ritual blessing alone, your thoughts and prayer power connect you with others.

PRACTICE/MEDITATION

I discovered the importance of silence at mealtime from patients at an eating disorder clinic where I worked as a Senior Mental Health Therapist. One day, while lunch was being handed out, a girl in the group asked if we could spend a minute meditating in silence before the meal—like I'd taught them to do in our group sessions. She explained it was helpful because, "It reduces our fear."

Frankly, I was there to make sure no one engaged in eating disordered behavior because the group struggled with high levels of anxiety around food and eating.

After sitting in silence for a minute, there seemed to be a greater calm in the room. You might think of silence as giving you a desire-free moment. It is a moment when the mind rests, when you can let loose of craving and desire and worry and yes, fear.

For today's meal, set an intention to be silent for a minute or even longer before eating. You might mentally state this in many ways, such as: "May I be silent," "May my silence invite peace," or "May my silence assist in freeing me from fear and anxiety with food." Phrase this however makes sense for you.

Spending time in silence is a beautiful ritual. It is a friend you can invite into each meal.

40

PREPARATION

Clean with Sacred Intent

*A Buddhist master once said, "The most
important thing in spiritual practice is food:
when you eat, how you eat, why you eat."*
—Lama Surya Das

Why is food such a wonderful spiritual practice? One reason is that food nourishes your body, spirit, and mind. But another important answer is that it brings you face to face with your physical desires. It is symbolic of the relationship you have with yourself, as well as a microcosm of the relationship you have with all things.

The struggle with food serves a positive purpose. It helps you find balance between your physical being on the one hand, and your spiritual nature on the other. It is through this struggle that you evolve and grow.

This is why all the wisdom traditions recognize that food can be used as a tool to unite your dual nature as a physical/spiritual being. This makes sense because food becomes part of you, part of your sacred spirit the moment you ingest it. For that reason, each moment of preparation is also sacred.

PRACTICE/MEDITATION

Today, you will bring a sacred mindset you're your preparation. Have you ever taken a sacred vow? Vows are statements we usually say in front of others as a way of declaring our love, respect, commitment, and values. Vows are an important way of demonstrating what you care about and what matters most in life. You might say that a vow takes something that could otherwise be viewed as mundane and elevates, or transforms it, into something deeply appreciated and viewed as sacred.

When the 6th century monk St. Benedict (see reading #26) asked his monks to "Regard all utensils and goods of the monastery as sacred vessels of the altar," he was instructing them to take a vow that transformed mundane objects into something special.

How would a vow of sacredness change your preparation? How would you care for the that sacred utensil, that sacred bowl, that sacred kitchen counter, and so on? How would you wash something that you viewed as sacred? How would you relish the opportunity to do so?

The opportunity to make this next preparation sacred is your for the taking. State your vow, and let your caring and respectful actions follow.

41

RITUAL

Add a Dash of Spontaneity to Blessings

Our Father (Mother) who art in heaven,
Hallowed be Thy name.
They Kingdom come,
They will be done, on earth, as it is in heaven.
Give us this day our daily bread.
—Traditional Christian Grace

Have you ever heard or recited grace such as the one noted above? I have experienced it when visiting friends or staying in various monasteries. There are many wonderful traditional ritual blessings such as this one that you can find for use in your own home or when you are out at a restaurant.

If you find one you like, should you stick with the same one over and over? How you use any ritual prayer or blessing is really up to you. Personally, I use a blessing that I have created which draws upon several traditions. At the same time, I vary it depending on the occasion, who is at the table, and so on.

When you allow yourself the freedom to try new blessings and phrases, you can bring what is happening in the moment into your prayers.

PRACTICE/MEDITATION

How spontaneous can you be with your blessing? As a practice, use a new blessing for each of today's meals. You might decide to extend your thoughts to those you don't know personally, but who you know are struggling. You could mention friends and others who are not physically in the space with you.

Also, you might decide to draw upon blessings from diverse traditions. If you're not familiar with such blessings, there are books that contain blessings from a host of different traditions. It can be fun to read and learn about these.

In addition, you might search for a spiritual reading from a teacher or favorite book that you like. If you're not sure what to do, you can always "let the spirit move you," allowing yourself to share what comes to mind in the moment.

42

PREPARATION

Discover the Hidden In-Between

After the recipe, I take a deep breath, relax,
and recall that I am in God's presence.
—Brother Rick Curry

In your journey of food, you would be mistaken if you thought the only transition time was before and after the meal. There is always time to reflect on what you are doing. Since you have to breathe anyway, why not take the time to take a conscious breath? In this way, there is always time to make a sacred connection.

In Christian monastic practice, there is something known as *statio*. This is often meant to denote the moment between moments, or the pause between those times when you are doing things. You can think of it as a mini-transition. You already experience this several times a day, such as when you are figuring out what to do next. Or, you take a momentary break to regroup.

With statio you make the pause intentional. Rest in the now moment. Take a single mindful, desire-free breath and recognize that there is no other time but this.

PRACTICE/MEDITATION

Awaken to the wonder of statio throughout your preparation time, as well as during your entire day.

So, what does the practice of statio look like? It looks like pausing for a moment, just putting things on simmer and not keeping the pot boiling! It means that you can feel your feet on the floor. That you can look out the window for a moment. That you can take a long slow breath as you gaze up at the unending blue sky. That you can watch a blade of grass grow (very slowly). That you can watch and smile at your children for no reason other than love. That you can pause while washing the dishes and feel the cool water splashing over your hands. That you can pause your hurt, anger, disappointment and frustration, knowing that these, too, are temporary and fleeting.

To take a sacred pause is to enter the timelessness of the moment. Find peace in your moment of statio. Feel the body that supports you. Notice the miracles of breath and air that give you life. Smallest thing you can in this moment. What is it?

Statio, that moment which is hidden, is also where the treasures are. Find them throughout the day. You might use your phone camera to snap pictures of them. Share the wonder of these statio moments with others. How glorious!

43

RITUAL

A Vow of Mindful Discipline

To develop a disciplined way of life,
you need to look at your own situation.
... At this point you are your own witness.
—Kalu Rinpoche, *The Dharma*

Rituals serve many purposes. They can put you in touch with spirit, break patterns by slowing you down, and help you gain discipline and strength.

There is a wonderful metaphor, used by Kalu Rinpoche and others, about two houses, each containing a treasure. One house can only be accessed through a single door, which is locked shut. The other house has an unlocked door and several windows, all of which are open. It is not hard to imagine which house will have its treasure stolen! How do you guard your true treasure—your one and only body and your precious awareness?

With ritual, you can safeguard these treasures. Each tradition has something you can use with a ritual to guard against mindless eating. Use what speaks to you.

PRACTICE/MEDITATION

With your ritual blessing, add a precept or vow of mindful discipline at today's meal. To start, consider using a vow just for a single meal or for the day. Vows of discipline are taken because they are helpful and beneficial.

For example, eating as much as you want of any foods without regard for the body and mind might feel great in the moment. But in the long term that is not a beneficial strategy. However, taking a vow to eat only what your body needs at today's meal could help train you to eat more healthfully. Or, you might decide not to consume an entire meal by taking a vow to leave something on the plate when you finish eating.

Here are some other vows which encourage discipline:

- A vow to eat when my hunger is in a moderate range.
- A vow to eat more slowly by chewing each bite fully.
- A vow to eat without distractions.

Rather than thinking of discipline as something that reduces choices, discipline is best understood as a means of training the mind and body. As written by Sufi master Inayat Khan, from *The Gayan*, "Freedom is not the path to freedom. Discipline is the path to freedom."

44

PREPARATION

Cooking with Love

*The most indispensable ingredient of all good
home cooking: love for those you are cooking for.*
—Sophia Loren

C an you recall any memorable meals from childhood? Do
you remember a special holiday time you had with those
you cared about? Such is the power of food cooked with
love.

Personally, for example, I can still feel the love from those
Sundays I spent at my grandparent's apartment in Chicago. My
extended family was present, including cousins and often a new
guest from out of town. But what really made the day special was the
food my grandmother prepared from scratch. Her freshly baked
apple pie and exotic eastern European foods—such as gefilte fish

and matzo ball soup—were the highlight of the night. I am certain the love my grandmother had for us went into that food.

How do you approach preparation and cooking? Think about those you are cooking for with love, and your whole meal can be infused with a sense of bliss, joyousness, and wholeness.

PRACTICE/MEDITATION

Prepare a meal or snack for yourself (and others) with love. One good way to begin this practice is by centering yourself with a loving-kindness meditation. This meditation primes your brain and body for trust and openness.

This ancient practice begins with first sending love to yourself. This is not a selfish kind of love or narcissism. If you have ever loved someone deeply (even a pet), then you know the kind of deep abiding wish for another's safety and well-being that I'm talking about. And so, you will begin by extending this warm love to your-self. Begin by sitting in silence, eyes closed, with a focus on your breathing. Now repeat the following words to yourself either out loud or inwardly:

May I be well.
May I be happy and healthy.
May I be at peace.
May I be free from pain, hunger, and suffering.

Keep repeating these words to yourself as many times as feels necessary. Let the feeling of love spread into all the cells of your body, even radiating into and from your heart.

Now, with this feeling of loving-kindness, prepare your meal. Let the feeling of love pour out into your food. You might even whisper, "May this food help others to be well, happy, healthy and peaceful."

45
RITUAL

Receive the Blessing that Awaits

For the more prayer is received,
rather than made,
the more genuine it will be.
—Thelma Hall, *Too Deep for Words*

Does your ritual blessing *receive* in the deepest sense? This question asks you to think about the difference between *making* a prayer and *receiving* one. Realize that this subtle distinction can have a real impact on how you eat and feel about your meal.

Your ritual blessing sets the stage for what follows. For example, if you *make* a blessing, then you are proactive and being in charge—just as when you take food. Taking in this fashion is often based on your physical needs, craving, and desires. On the other hand, when you *receive* a blessing, then you tap into a bigger process. You offer yourself up to the mercy and grace of the divine. You accept what is given with a great and open heart. It follows then, that you open yourself to receiving food in this same way—letting it come to you without greed, desire, and hunger.

By shifting your blessing toward receiving, you can slowly but surely transform emotional hunger and greed into sacred eating and accepting. You can *take* food, or you can *receive* it.

PRACTICE/MEDITATION

Sit in spacious silence. Open yourself to receiving a mealtime blessing. Receiving in this sense can be considered as a means of volitionally surrendering oneself to the moment. Make no mistake, though. Surrender in this context is not submission.

Submission means that one is forced to give up their own free will and choice, whether by force or other means. In contrast, surrender signifies a process of giving up what keeps one rigidly stuck in place. To surrender means to release the ego's demands and needs; it is the essence of humility.

How can you humble yourself to whatever this next meal has to offer? Removing the ego at mealtime is a blessing unto itself. Let yourself eat in an unadorned way. You need no words here. Simply accepting the sacredness of eating is more than enough.

Humble yourself before the gift of energy and life that is being offered. How sublime!

46

PREPARATION

Be Mindful of Even the Smallest Detail

*It is imperative for the tenzo to actively involve
himself personally in both the selection
and the preparation of the ingredients.*
—Soei Yoneda

The *tenzo*, or cook, of a monastery does not prepare haphazardly. He is mindful of every little detail. Even the amount of food required for a meal is to be calculated to the grain of rice!

How involved and mindful are you in the meals you prepare at home?

Even if the extent of your preparation is placing a packaged meal in the oven, you do so with great attention to detail. How closely, for example, do you read the instructions? Do you ever question or wonder about any of the ingredients? How much food do you waste through preparation? Remember that it is okay to question, to doubt, to learn more.

The more connected you become to the source of food, the more involved you are in the preparation and ultimately, the eating.

PRACTICE/MEDITATION

For today's practice, you will take a more active role in preparation of today's meal through increased awareness and mindfulness of every little detail.

The importance of setting intentions and staying embodied during preparation were mentioned earlier (#28). Sense the body as you move about. In addition, pay particular to the ingredients in your food. If the food is processed, how many of the listed items are natural or understandable? How much unnecessary sugar does each processed food item contain? Sugar, in various forms, is added to many foods and recipes. You might reflect on what healthy alternatives or substitutes can be used instead of sugar when cooking.

Finally, how closely can you follow the recipe directions for either preparing or cooking your meal? Some foods require boiling, simmering and stirring. Others need to be sautéed or baked. Do you have the right oils, pans, utensils and measuring tools for the job? If not, what would work best?

Even if you can't make changes in your meal today, your reflections about ingredients and cooking methods can help you make positive changes in the future.

47

RITUAL

Express Your Spirit through Food

*We can eat for our bodies
or we can eat for our souls.
Sabbath eating is to delight in our food,
feasting, and not merely eating.*
—Donna Schaper, *Sabbath Keeping*

P erhaps you have noticed that the wisdom traditions have several things in common to connect with the divine, such as ritual cleansing and prayer at mealtime. Some, like the Hindu and Indian traditions, focus on the idea of hospitality by putting the emphasis on sharing food during festivities and showing respect to guests.

How do you "eat for your soul"? Do you have a favorite mode (perhaps "a la mode") of expressing your spirit through food? Even if you live alone (or with others), you can show hospitality by giving away unused food—to a hungry person or the neighborhood critters and pets. Leftovers and even spoiled food make for good compost so you can create more food, more abundance.

When you think about it, everything gets recycled sooner or later. You are just recycling mindfully.

PRACTICE/MEDITATION

What could nourish you as a new way to "eat for your soul." We're not just talking about food here, but also *how* and *where* and *who* might be included in order to turn your meal into a true feast, one that *fulfills you* instead of one that just *fills you up*.

This is an opportunity for you to conjure up and savor a special food that is connected to cherished memories. Maybe it's a food you haven't eaten in a long time, or maybe it's lovingly making that one-of-a-kind recipe given to you by a dear family member.

To nourish your soul, you can also think about how to celebrate a meal at meaningful place, such as at city, festival or restaurant where you experienced a special event in your life?

Who can join in your celebration and feast? Whether you eat alone or with others, what's important is how you express this meal. If others are there, let them know their presence is special and appreciated.

48

PREPARATION

Be a Meal Architect

Maintain an attitude that tries to build
great temples from ordinary greens.
—13th century Zen Master Dogen

id you ever make a meal that was, to put it gently, a flop? These humbling experiences prove one thing. You are human. A perfect omelet is not mastered in a day.

The preparation stage lets you make even simple food exceptional, as Zen Master Dogen advises. When you thoughtlessly slap together a meal, you might miss the opportunity to add some extra touch that would have made that sandwich (salad, soup, dessert) special.

That's why presentation is a key ingredient to any meal. Whether you eat alone or with others, you can add a touch of artistry and effort into your meal. And, even if your meal comes in a prepackaged container, you can decide how to beautifully arrange the contents on plates along with other foods.

﹅

PRACTICE/MEDITATION

By utilizing skillful presentation and preparation, you can transform an ordinary meal into something special. As a first step, visualize what you hope to create. Whether you're making an omelet, a salad or a hamburger, you can imagine the meal's scent, look, and taste even before you start.

Next, imagine that you are not just the cook, but the architect of this food "temple," or meal. What tastes, flavors and colors would accentuate the basic omelet, salad or hamburger?

Naturally, an architect understands the tools of the trade. They know how design and materials work together. Realize that your own time spent in the kitchen has given you much expertise as well!

Take a moment to imagine how a lightly toasted bun, cheddar cheese, and a slice of lettuce and tomato can change the appearance and flavor of something like a basic burger.

Use your vast storehouse of memory to go beyond your normal methods, routines, and recipes. If you don't have all the ingredients available at this time, you can bring your flavor design ideas into a future meal.

Do one thing that sets this meal apart from how you have presented or prepared it in the past. Now, enjoy!

49

RITUAL

Integrate Intention and Action

When you have total intention to create something . . .
it simply cannot fail to manifest.
—Shakti Gawain, *Creative Visualization*

With ritual, you can create and use an intention that specifically states your daily commitment to eat a better diet, achieve health, and lose excess weight, etc. In this way, your ritual blessing serves a practical purpose—to actualize your deepest hopes and desires through intention. (If you want, your intention can extend beyond mealtime issues and into other areas of your life.)

First, make a commitment to say a ritual before each meal. Then, you will want to follow what Shakti Gawain describes as the following three steps: "that is you deeply desire it, you completely believe that you can do it, and you are totally willing to have it." To help you stay disciplined, repeat your intention at each meal.

But you still need to be skillful in your choices for the long term. If you stumble from cheesecake to cheesecake and never exercise, the intention of being healthy will not, by itself, be enough to materialize a healthy body.

❧

PRACTICE/MEDITATION

Create a desire with your total intention, then follow up with skillful action. When making intentional changes to your life, whether related to food or otherwise, it can be helpful to think in terms of *small*, *realistic* and *achievable*.

Why do these three words matter? That's because, without them, you might set yourself up for failure and as a result lose steam and enthusiasm. Let's suppose I want to run a marathon, but have never run before. If I set the intention of running a marathon and decide to start with training by running 10 miles a day, I'll probably get disappointed and stop. But if I set *small*, *realistic* and *achievable* goals that back up my larger intention, then I can build upon success one small step at a time.

So if your intention is to lose weight or get healthier, you'll want to define small steps that can get you closer to those intentions. That might mean reducing certain foods from your diet, adding other foods, exercising more often, and so on. This fosters a moderate approach, not a diet-centered all-or-none way of thinking or acting.

As Shakti Gawain advises, deeply desire your intention, believe you can attain it, and then totally act on behalf of it. Only do so moderately, in a manner that is gentle and filled with love and self-compassion.

50

PREPARATION

Make a Seasonal Shift

Life is not hurrying on to a receding future,
nor hankering after the imagined past.
It is the turning aside like Moses
to the miracle of the lit bush.
—Prayer from the Celtic Tradition

I n the Northern Hemisphere, the Vernal Equinox marks the beginning of Spring on or around March 20 or 21. With each yearly springtime cycle comes new hope, growth, life, activity, possibility, transformation, and vitality. Each season brings a different emphasis and shift.

What season do you find yourself in at right now? Is there a seasonal shift or transformation you can introduce into your daily preparation? Maybe you can make a shift in emotional attachment, such as letting go of negative emotions around food and eating. Or, perhaps you can prepare your table and dining space in a way that is in harmony with the ideals of a particular season.

PRACTICE/MEDITATION

Bring the energy of the season into your preparation. As the seasons shift you can be more mindful of the foods your body craves as it adapts to seasonal changes. Find balance and harmony between your body and nature by preparing ingredients that you know to be pure and fresh and seasonal.

Some good spring foods, for example, include wild mushrooms, corn, cherry tomatoes, and strawberries. For the summer season, veggies and fruits of all kinds abound, including cucumbers, cauliflower, broccoli, peppers and lettuce. The autumn season graces us with such delectable items as pumpkins, Brussels sprouts, pears and squash. Winter is a good season for hearty stews and comforting soups containing kale, carrots, garlic, beets, cabbage and more.

If you are unsure, ask your local produce manager what foods are seasonal.

STEP 3
EATING AND COMMUNITY

The essential mealtime elements of eating and community are intrinsically woven together. Recognizing and honoring both will bring a new sense of meaning, harmony and gratitude into each bite. Discover how the practices and meditations in this section uplift and lighten body, mind and spirit.

51

COMMUNITY

Invite Curiosity and Connection

No heaven can come to us unless
our hearts find rest in today.
Take Heaven!
—Fra Giovanni, 16th century Italian Architect

When you eat for emotional reasons or even out of boredom, it may be a sign that you seek greater meaning or connection in your meals—and your lives. Mealtime rituals offer fulfillment by showing you the divine nature and order of all things, visible and invisible.

This is illustrated in the story of a man who once searched for heaven on Earth.

"I have looked for angels," he said, "but I have yet to see one. I have looked for miracles, but never found anything worthy of God."

His neighbor, however, saw heaven everywhere he turned.

"I hear the angels singing in the wind that blows through the fields of wheat," he said, "and the miracle of God in each fruit and vegetable that sustains my life."

PRACTICE/MEDITATION

Have you let boredom seep into your mealtime? Have you forgotten how you found wonder in so many new things as a child?

For this meditation, you will call upon your childlike curiosity to seek out the extraordinary as you invite new connections and meaning into today's meal.

To begin, find a place where you can rest in quiet without inter-ruption. Reflect back on a time in your childhood when your curiosity peaked. What enthralled you? What captured your imag-ination?

Allow yourself to feel how that sense of curiosity, wonder, and awe felt in your body and throughout your being. Maybe you felt tingly, giggly or giddy? Whatever that sensation was, let it infuse you now. Imagine how you might bring this feeling into today's meal.

That might mean spending time looking at the wonder of nature while eating. It could mean inviting someone new to share lunch or dinner with you. It could mean having fun with some new food choices to get explore and get curious about.

The good news is that you can always come back to that childlike feeling of wonder and curiosity. This will always be with you and a part of you. How marvelous!

52

EATING

Bring Moderation to Each Bite

Patience ... moderation in food ...
[and] striving for spiritual advancements
is the teaching of all Buddhas.
—The Buddha

Have you ever found it difficult to eat with patience and moderation? If so, you are not alone. And so, you need to ask, what is patience with food? What does it mean to eat moderately?

If you find that you often eat quickly, eat too much, or ignore food's importance by putting it off until the last moment, then you may find that patience and moderation with food are missing ingredients for creating a truly fulfilling meal.

You may also have a "secret food" that is caused by secret emotional cravings. You might ask, "Why is this food/emotion a secret for me?" Because such foods hold an emotional charge, we might find moderation difficult—and as a result, we may either restrict or overindulge in that food. Patience and moderation offer a middle path between the extremes of overindulgence and denial.

PRACTICE/MEDITATION

The first step toward moderation is simply noticing when you are *not* patient and moderate, especially when it comes to food cravings and desires. Instead of *reacting to the craving or desire*, you can *respond by observing the craving or desire*. Here's how you can watch it, investigate it, and examine it closely.

Take a moment to consciously breathe in and out. Then simply notice the craving or desire by naming or labeling it, "this is craving." Now, note the intensity of the craving on a 1-10 scale (1=no craving to 10=extreme craving). Notice where you feel the craving in the body —such as the head, the gut, etc. Lastly, give an emotional name to the feeling. For example, the craving might not really be physical, but emotional. It might be loneliness, sadness, frustration, stress, hurt, disappointment, and so on. Allow yourself as much time as you need to complete this process.

When done, you might return again to rate the intensity on a 1-10 scale. It's not uncommon for the intensity to fall after observing cravings in this way. Finish by exhaling out any negative tension and craving, letting your breath carrying it out, down the body and out the bottom of your feet and depositing it back into the Earth for recycling.

Instead of being in the grip of the desire or craving, you have made it the object of your attention! After this practice, let yourself eat more at peace and moderately.

53

COMMUNITY

Find Joy in the Great Chain of Being

For it is in giving that we receive.
—Saint Francis of Assisi, *A Simple Prayer*

Each meal, each morsel is a gift. That is why—even if you are single and eat many meals by yourself—you never really eat alone. Consider for a moment, how each meal brings you into communion with the community at large.

The Earth provides a bounty of food. Farmers plant seeds and harvest crops. Truckers transport food to local distribution centers. Retailers stock the shelves.

This great chain of being and giving never sleeps.

That you are part of a community and planet that shares food is one of the amazing gifts of being. In the broader sense, is not each meal—indeed, everything in your life—something that is given?

This is true even when you work for your meals—because even one's livelihood can be viewed as a blessing.

PRACTICE/MEDITATION

It can be a major mind shift to realize how each foodstuff connects us to our planet and community. Here are just a few questions to consider. You might apply these to your own meal or the foods you choose to eat today.

- How much sunlight is in each cherry tomato or cucumber slice on your plate?
- How much water is needed to grow that almond that is in your salad?
- What is it like to pick strawberries off the vine without bruising them?

How easy is it to forget the myriad of little steps and the great chain of being that are necessary to bring quality food to our plates. Have you ever visited a farm or worked with the soil? When we return to the fields from which life springs forth—even for a short visit—the link between mindful eating and the Earth's ecological wellness becomes a little more visible. You can always meditate on these wise words:

Whatever befalls the earth,
Befalls the sons and daughters of the earth.
—Ted Perry (inspired by Chief Seattle), *how can one sell the air*

54

EATING

Taste Like a Food Genius

The full use of taste is an act of genius.
—John La Farge, artist

The full use of taste is not only genius. It is miraculous. The enzyme amylase, which is present in saliva, begins to digest carbohydrates as you grind and chew your food. Chewing also breaks food into smaller pieces that come into contact with the taste buds.

How many times do you chew? There is no right answer. In mindfulness training, Buddhist monks practice chewing food from twenty-five to one hundred times prior to swallowing. The more attention you place on chewing the more you will taste your food with greater intensity and bliss.

This practice is best done in silence. Begin with something small, like a raisin, a grape, an almond, or a slice of orange. Take small bites.

Be mindful as you chew, noticing how each food's taste and consistency keeps changing. Expect the unexpected.

PRACTICE/MEDITATION

For this practice, you will imagine that you have never eaten or tried food before. But you have heard that humans love food, and so you want to try some of it out for yourself. With this open mindset, you will take part in a mindful eating practice. To begin, find a small portion of food from which you can take at least three bites. This could be an orange slice, a piece of chocolate, a cookie or cracker, or even something as small as a raisin. After you've got your food, have a seat and place it in the palm of your hand.

Observe all you can about your chosen food. How symmetrical is it? What color or colors does it contain? If it has a stem (such as a raisin, grape or strawberry), notice the shape and color of the stem. How heavy is it? You might raise it up and down to sense the weight.

Next, raise the food up to your nose. With your eyes closed, see what it smells like? Finally, imagine what is "in" this food? How much sunlight, rainwater and soil nutrients does it contain?

Now, take a small bite, paying attention to the texture and flavor. The mouth has over 10,000 taste buds. There are even taste buds on the roof of the mouth. Can you taste this food on the roof of your mouth? Where on the tongue is the flavor most intense? Least intense?

Keep chewing until the food is liquid. Then, set the intention to swallow. As you do, can you follow the food all the way down the esophagus and into the stomach?

Repeat this process with the next two bites. See how the taste changes from bite to bite. And, see if you can chew 20-25 times before intentionally swallowing.

55

COMMUNITY

Practice Forgiveness During Mealtime

Forgiveness is to offer no resistance to life—
to allow life to live through you.
The alternatives are pain and suffering . . .
—Eckhart Tolle, *The Power of Now*

What does it mean to forgive at mealtime? If you hold a grudge during a meal, it will affect how you eat. If you are tense then you may eat more quickly and chew less, which will affect your digestion. If you are upset with someone during mealtime—whether or not they are present—you may stop listening to your body's signals and eat more (or less) food than you need.

Forgiving, like eating, is a healing and nourishing experience. If you hold a grudge or anger toward another, then you are only continuing your suffering. What are you holding onto?

Mealtime is a good time to learn to let forgive and let go. The food on your table gives itself to you voluntarily. Your ritual blessing forgives you for your own mistakes. After all, who has not erred in life?

❧

PRACTICE/MEDITATION

To forgive is to let go of anger, even a little. Begin by reflecting on the following: To forgive at the dinner table asks us to wipe the slate clean and start anew. This is not to suggest that you simply forget, but that you forgive while still remembering.

To forgive yourself for hurts you may have caused others—as well as forgiving others for the hurts they may have caused you—is a powerful gift to oneself. Learning to let go of what does not serve us, or others, is one way of releasing the baggage we are holding on to.

Letting go of what ensnares us is one purpose of forgiveness, isn't it? It can be helpful to take the sage advice of Nelson Mandela, who wrote, "Thinking too well of people often allows them to be better than they otherwise would." If you can forgive and think well of others, why not also think the best of yourself?

It all adds up to the central and lasting teachings we can receive from forgiveness: To recognize that no one is perfect.

Breathe in forgiveness for yourself, then breathe it out for all beings who have erred and could benefit from the healing salve of forgiveness.

EATING

Be Your Own "First Guest"

*In all circumstances serenity of mind should be
maintained, and conversation should be conducted
as never to mar the harmony of the surroundings.*
—Kakuzo Okakura, *The Book of Tea*

I n the tea ceremony, there is someone who is called the "first guest." This person's responsibility is to ease the flow of conversation and sociability of the occasion. Other guests take part, too, admiring ancient tea kettles and cups that are used in the ceremony.

Everyone who is present for the tea ceremony recognizes the care and effort that has gone into preserving these timeless antiques and preparing a beautiful tea room with a theme appropriate to the celebration. The result is a sense of wholeness. Can you hope to accomplish this same sublime process in your home or at any meal?

The next time you are a guest, take time to look around. Appreciate the effort and surroundings of your host. Let your words and actions facilitate a sense of oneness and harmony.

PRACTICE/MEDITATION

Here are some ways that you can serve as "first guest" at your next meal and bring in unifying concepts from the Japanese tea ceremony known as "the Way of Tea." This approach follows the four main values of harmony, purity, respect and tranquility, and it means looking at the kitchen, meal, guests, and hosts in an entirely new way. Through practicing these four principles, you complete what is incomplete—within yourself and the world around you.

With harmony all the guests unite in a space that is buffered from external chaos. Guests recognize their sacred role in helping to maintain a sense of harmony.

With the principle of purity, all aspects of the meal highlight cleanliness and simplicity. This is purity that goes beyond cleanliness to include purity of thought and being.

The principle of respect means honoring others through words and actions, as well as having a sense of humility for the whole meal.

Through the principle of tranquility you learn to reduce your own ego needs and personal opinions in order to feel tranquility and peace in the presence of others.

As first guest, you can prepare and design a meal that is both steeped in beauty and conducive to social interaction. You could integrate heirloom or family items into the table setting, making sure to point these out. You might facilitate the sharing of stories, or create a unique theme for the meal. Tranquil music or lighting can go far in helping promote a sense of peace, togetherness and unity. Even giving guests a role in cleaning up or concluding the meal is in keeping with the spirit of the Way of Tea.

57

COMMUNITY

Open to Your Compassionate Voice

If you want others to be happy, practice compassion.
If you want to be happy, practice compassion.
—Dalai Lama

Much food-related unhappiness comes from not accepting the way things are. This plays out in many ways: "Why can't I look as good as (him/her)?" "Why can't I lose weight/stay on my diet and wear a size (fill in the blank)?" If you are stuck in that place, how can you ever hope to find happiness?

You can begin by practicing compassion for yourself and your own suffering. Compassion does not mean sympathy or pity, where you feel superior to another. The word *compassion* comes from Latin, meaning "together with" (*com*) "suffering" (*passion*). This is true empathy that brings you closer to understanding and loving yourself. When you are kinder to yourself, you can more easily accept, understand and extend compassion to others.

PRACTICE/MEDITATION

For this meditation, you will inwardly witness your own food suffering without judgment, blame or shame. From this vantage point, you can bring wisdom to bear on your situation.

Find a quiet place to sit for reflection where you won't be interrupted. Set the intention to observe your own food struggles without judgment.

As you sit, let yourself replay times when you have struggled with food. What that looks like and feels like—both before and after. If you can, name the emotions that are entangled with the experience.

As you do this, imagine breathing in a pure white light of compassion and understanding. Visualize this light coming in through the top of your head and spreading throughout your entire body, from the top of your head, down your torso, spine, internal organs, and traveling all the way down your legs and into your feet.

For a few moments, feel yourself bathed in this cleansing light of compassion for your food struggles.

Now, set the intention to connect with your wise, compassionate self, or voice. Don't force this, and release any expectation that the compassionate voice will answer. Simply open yourself to that inner compassionate voice. What would your wise voice say to you that brings empathy, warmth, forgiveness and understanding? You can have a dialogue with your compassionate voice as well. When you're done, give thanks to this supportive part of you. How beautiful!

58

EATING

Explore the Just-ness of Each Moment

Tea is nought but this:
First you heat the water,
Then you make the tea.
Then you drink it properly,
That is all you need to know.
—Sen Rikyu, 16th century tea master

Did you ever experience a tea ceremony? I once had the opportunity to attend a full-fledged Japanese tea ceremony that consisted of thick tea, or *matcha*, thin tea, and a complete meal. Traditionally, the tea ceremony is very ceremonial, with special ways of handling utensils and wiping off the tea cup, and so on. Honestly, I was worried that I would embarrass myself and the host. However, my fears were unfounded. Tea, like any meal, only asks that you be aware of each little movement of your body and everything before you. This is mindfulness, and with this little secret you can find moment-to-moment oneness with anything—especially food. While you eat, simply pay attention with bare awareness. With bare awareness, a banana is not yellow, curved, and sweet. It just *is*. Use bare awareness to experience food in a new way.

PRACTICE/MEDITATION

Just-ness at mealtime means being present with just this bite, just this chewing, just this swallowing, and so on—without altering the bare experience. In Practice/Meditation #54, you experienced the just-ness of taste. Here, you'll broaden out your awareness to experience all of the tiniest details of eating. That means you can notice how your jaw and mouth open to receive each bite. You can notice how tightly or loosely your hands and fingers hold onto food or utensils. You can turn awareness toward how fast or slow you chew. You can also bring conscious decision-making into the eating process. For example, you can choose where and how large a bite to take of that next morsel.

With bare awareness, you are not adding or subtracting from the experience. There is just you, chewing, eating, swallowing, digesting, and noticing hunger and satiety cues. To eat like this means noticing judgments and releasing them.

just-ness is a wonderful way to learn more about yourself and your connection to food and eating. There is no craving for food here, there is just nourishing the body. just-ness also takes emotional blame and worry out of the equation. If you notice negativity, simply name the thought or the emotion. Then, return to being present with the next chew, the next bite and the next selection.

This just-ness eating meditation may slow you down, so notice how it alters old eating habits and patterns.

59

COMMUNITY

Gratitude for Today's Food Journey

A kitchen condenses the universe.
—Betty Fussell, *My Kitchen Wars*

The journey of food begins long, long before it appears sanitized, frozen, processed, prepared and packaged neatly on your grocery shelves. Food all begins alive in the world, swimming in rivers and oceans, grazing on ranches, growing on trees, and ripening in farms and fields.

Too often we think of food just as any manufactured product, when in truth it is organic and of the Earth, like all of us. If you really think about it, the wholeness of food is dependent on an entire community that is responsible for getting food to our table.

Then, there are those who distribute and ship the food to our local communities. The effort is massive and seamless, which is why

is it easy for many of us—unlike those living in places less fortunate
—to take our bounty for granted.

⁏🐚

PRACTICE/MEDITATION

Today you will reflect on the individuals who made your meal possible, and appreciate them and the Earth that sustains life.

You can start, for example, by looking at the food on your plate. What was the journey of each particular food? Can you imagine where it was farmed and harvested? Nowadays, many fruits and vegetables—such as various greens, tomatoes, oranges, apples and bananas—are available throughout the year because they can be shipped from faraway countries where the growing season differs from ours.

You might give thanks to all those persons and services that made this food possible. Food is a basic necessity like water, shelter and warmth. Without any of these, life might be impossible or an extreme hardship.

You may even consider how this food helps you complete your own personal journey, today and tomorrow. Knowing how precious the food on your plate really is, can you eat in a way that honors and respects the community that is contained within each item on your plate.

60

EATING

Notice Habits and Daily Food Static

Giving up smoking is the easiest thing in the world.
I know because I've done it thousands of times.
—Mark Twain

I s there a food habit that you really, really want to change? The power of desire can be so strong that it sometimes keeps us bound in a habitual behavior. So, what is the secret to changing any habit? The first step is acknowledgment and acceptance of our own habits, without trying to judge them. Having acceptance and tolerance for our inner desires is a good place from which to initiate change.

One beneficial and powerful starting point is to recognize "food static" in your life. Just as static interrupts a clear signal on a phone, TV or radio, food static gets in the way of clarity and making the best choices for your long term health.

Food static, for instance, could be anything from tempting food at the market and mouth-watering advertisements to all those "cookies" (metaphorical or literal) that confront you at work, during the holidays or at other times.

PRACTICE/MEDITATION

For this practice, you will bring your attention to the food static that surrounds you on a daily basis. To begin, set your intention to notice all the food static that foils you from making clear and deliberate choices.

Once your intention is firmly in place, you can start to notice which foods, stressors and thoughts act as negative triggers that stimulate old habits, emotions and cravings. As you do this, be kind and compassionate with yourself, knowing that you are not forcing change, but simply being more aware.

When encountering food static, take long and slow deep breaths. Allow yourself to be accepting of how you are responding to the static. Acceptance also means that you can be at peace with the static. You may not have control over all forms of advertisements and food static, but you do have control over how you respond.

Which each exhale, feel your body relax a little bit more. You might even imagine that you are breathing out the offending food static. Let your breath carry the impulse caused by food static to travel down the body. You can even deposit the static out the bottom of your feet and back into the earth for recycling.

By simply noticing food static and accepting it, you have changed your old habitual response to it. Smile inwardly at your new choice!

61

COMMUNITY

The Gift of Deep Listening

*To truly listen to another is a main course
of the family's inner meal.*
—Donald Altman, *Art of the Inner Meal*

Meals can heal. When you were a child and teenager, did you have a chance to speak freely, to contribute and to be heard at mealtime? Such is the potential of a healing meal. To truly listen to others is to witness and understand your family's story—or community's story, as the case may be.

But where do you begin? The first step, as with all mindfulness, is to gain awareness of *what is*. Just observe and learn. Is everyone fighting for the last word? Or, maybe no one speaks except to say, "pass the potatoes."

If you eat alone, you can also open yourself to the sounds of what is around you at mealtime. Listening is a both a gift and birthright.

PRACTICE/MEDITATION

For your next meal with others, you will take the role of a kind and willing listener. Set your intention to deeply listen at the meal. You could even set the intention to learn one new thing about each person who joins you at the table. Even if you know someone, deep listening can offer a fresh and profound view into the life and feelings of others.

Each time you feel like interrupting, take a calming in-breath and out-breath as you let others speak. This is a perfect time for you to be like a detective as you observe interactions at mealtime. Listening is more than just being quiet. It means that you are actively absorbing what others are saying. The acronym **H.E.A.R.** from my book *Clearing Emotional Clutter* describes the four steps involved in deep listening. These steps include:

1) *Hold All Assumptions*—let go of your beliefs and assumptions for the moment in order to make space for the ideas of others.

2) *Enter Others' Emotional World*—use empathy to help you understand another's world and personal point of view.

3) *Absorb and Accept the Messages of Others*—let the message of others sink in so that you can better understand and accept their perspective instead of just seeing them one dimensionally as "good" or "bad."

4) *Reflect First, Then Respond with Respect*—if you are feeling anger, do not respond in the moment. Give yourself time to reflect and only respond when you can do so respectfully.

The H.E.A.R. method doesn't mean you must agree with the ideas of others. Rather, it means you can better know where others are coming from as you foster mutual understanding and peace.

Is deep listening easy to do? No, but your exploration will help you discover more about its hidden ability to heal wounds and nurture greater understanding.

62

EATING

Eating Your Forbidden Food

I call on a dream that reminds us
to focus on our fingertips,
on the shape and weight of our hand
on blood and bone and a thousand nerve endings
as we raise an apple to our mouths.
—Oriah Mountain Dreamer, author

Have you ever forgotten a meal shortly after you ate it? Fortunately, mindfulness focuses the attention on every little detail of sight, taste, movement, smell, and hearing. This way, you can never forget how miraculous it is to simply bite into an apple!

An entire network of interconnected synapses navigates your hand with its sensitive nerves toward the apple. Your optic nerve sends upside down images of the apple to the brain (where the images are translated). Your olfactory senses are some of the body's most ancient sensing equipment. As your taste buds send messages to your pleasure centers, the hearing apparatus picks up the vibrations of your chewing.

A myriad of involuntary systems work simultaneously, as you breathe and digest. Revel in this master orchestration the next time you bite into an apple, or even the food that triggers overeating.

PRACTICE/MEDITATION

For today's meditation, you will experience a "forbidden" food over which you may have little control. You will use the same mindful eating tools practiced earlier. Set a designated time for how long you want to eat your forbidden or binge food without any distractions. Make sure all electrical devices are turned off.

Have you ever wondered what would it be like to eat your forbidden food with extreme mindfulness? Occasionally, I have had clients eat their "binge" food very slowly and mindfully. One client, a woman who normally stress binged on potato chips, had a completely different experience after mindfully taking very tiny bites and chewing many times before swallowing. In fact, after six minutes she ate only two chips. When I said the exercise was over, she responded, "Oh thank God! I couldn't eat another chip."

Another client ate his binge cookie mindfully over the course of several minutes. When finished, he exclaimed, "I thought these cookies were good, but now that I've *really* tasted them, I don't ever want another."

As you intentionally chew, taste, and swallow, notice how this changes your experience. What new things have you learned or discovered?

63

COMMUNITY

Share Your Wealth with a G.L.A.D. Story

*Storytelling is a way of giving someone
great and lasting wealth.*
—Joseph Bruchac, Native American storyteller

Chances are you have heard (and shared) some fascinating stories with others over food. Isn't this a wonderful way to get to know another? In truth, we are constantly telling and retelling the story of who we are—as a global community, a country, a culture, a city, a neighborhood, a family, and as individuals.

For example, history (his-story and her-story) contains many perspectives and myths. Is any single version correct? Don't you get a fuller and more complete story when you share and hear all sides of another's situation? Even if you eat dinner alone while watching TV, you can watch the news or any show from a more spacious point of view.

PRACTICE/MEDITATION

For today's practice, you will share the story of your day with others. And, you will elicit and hear the stories of others with openness and nonjudgment. Keep in mind that when we share our stories, we are making sense of our world, our experiences and what matters to us.

There are many ways to elicit stories beyond simply asking, "how was your day?" Here is an acronym that can stimulate rich stories for your family or others who you share meals with. The **G.L.A.D. Practice** (from my books *The Mindfulness Toolbox* and *Simply Mindful Resilience*) is designed to get you out of your head and into appreciating those often overlooked gems of daily life.

G stands for *gratitude*. This could be the story of one thing you (or others) are grateful for today. In addition, make sure you explain *why* you are grateful, because sharing the *why* deepens and enriches the story.

L stands for *learning*. What one thing did you learn today? Maybe you learned something new about yourself, about another, or just learned something new that you were curious about.

A stands for *accomplishment*. What one thing did you accomplish today? Remember that the small things count. This can include anything from a small act of self-care like getting enough sleep to taking an action that gets you one step closer to an important goal.

D stands for *delight*. What one thing brought you a sense of joy today? Perhaps you saw a beautiful flower, shared a laugh with another, or enjoyed exercising.

Whatever you share, enjoy the process of opening and learning about others through their stories.

64

EATING

Experiencing Silence from the Gods

We learn speech from men,
silence from the gods.
—Plutarch

Have you ever *consciously* eaten a meal in silence? This practice has been a part of many monastic practices for centuries. One reason why this is useful is that you can more easily focus attention on your meal and on the mindfulness surrounding it, such as your breath.

Do you breathe while you eat? When I have asked this question of participants in Mindfulness Workshops, many of them have no idea. Silence makes it easier to concentrate on how you breathe, chew, swallow, and how the taste and texture of food changes in your mouth. It even lets you focus on how certain flavors fill you with desire for more food.

Now, if you are frightened of the idea of being silent, it's understandable. After all, we live in a culture where silence is almost unheard of. Noise and sounds buzz around all the time—especially the noise of our own thoughts! This practice will help you understand that silence can be a friend, not something to fear.

PRACTICE/MEDITATION

For today's mindful eating meditation, you can set the intention to sit in silence for five or ten minutes as you eat. If that's too long, try one or two minutes. Silence doesn't mean you won't have thoughts. Of course you will! Silence in this context only means that you are making space for mindful eating awareness.

You can also do this with others who agree to sit in silence for the first five minutes of the meal. The idea here is to replace talking with attentiveness. When you are silently eating, you can also be more aware of others, including their needs. For example, if you notice someone needs something, such as more water or food, you can offer that to them. Also, you might feel the presence of others more strongly when you eat silently with them.

Keep in mind that research shows that most people tend to overeat while distracted. But here, sitting in silence, distraction is kept to a minimum. There's just you, your food and the other person(s) getting nutrition.

While eating, you could decide to take a conscious breath between bites. Chew up to twenty times or more before swallowing. Experience silence, breathing, and chewing during the meal, as well as the appreciation for others with whom you share this sacred time.

Eating in silence can also be a good practice for slowing down at mealtime because you'll naturally be more aware of the pace of your eating.

65

COMMUNITY

Invite Patience and Forbearance

First, do no harm.
—Hippocrates

The Greek doctor Hippocrates, who is considered the "Father of Medicine," developed the first medical code of ethics and is known for his Hippocratic Oath. His suggestion to "first, do no harm" is central in all traditions and is vital to how we relate to our community. So then, how can we do no harm at mealtime?

First, we can take steps to ensure that our meal does not become a battlefield where anger and negative emotion boil over. This does not mean we should cover up our feelings.

What it does mean, though, is that we can try to show respect and patience toward those with whom we share a meal. This is not always easy. Patience and forbearance are in danger of becoming lost arts. To practice them is to sow the seeds of peace and nonharm at mealtime.

Even if we eat alone, we need patience and forbearance for ourselves—this is also a form of doing no harm that lessens our own mental battles.

PRACTICE/MEDITATION

As you sit down for today's meal, set the intention to invite patience and forbearance into your meal space. What does this mean in terms of the actual mealtime? All things in life are subject to frailty and change. At home or at a restaurant, the food doesn't always come out as planned. A food item gets overdone; a cherished family dish falls and breaks into pieces; a difficult conversation threatens to derail dinnertime peace.

Any host of events, known and unknown, can occur. With patience, we can let go of our expectations of how we believe or want things to be. Forbearance goes a step further, because it involves our conscious decision to pause and not engage with others—especially at those times when the actions and words of others feel egregious to us. This is a form of giving grace to another. In other words, as Hippocrates recommends, we can choose to do no harm. The principle of causing "no harm" to other beings is embedded in the Indian traditions of Jainism, Hinduism, Buddhism and Sikhism. Ahimsa was a guiding ethical light for Gandhi, who embraced a nonviolent approach to social change.

When you decide to exhibit patience and forbearance into your meal space, you are aligning with a deep spiritual practice. How sublime!

66

EATING

What's Your New Flavor?

Life can only be created by life;
health only comes from an integration of
our various levels of function—not from
the intake of manufactured pills and potions.
—Annemarie Colbin, *Food and Healing*

O ur bodies are not machines, although we sometimes think of them in a mechanistic way. Rather, I like to think of the body as a divine vehicle holding the inseparable parts of our physical form (body), mind, and spirit. Tugging on the strings of any one of these parts cannot help but to move the others. If we ingest food that is not beneficial for our body, then it will likewise affect the ability of our mind and spirit to operate optimally.

Spiritual teachers know that food—as well as breath, exercises, prayer, and fasting—can be used to attain spiritual growth. That is why it can benefit us to make a list of those foods we think would be our "ideal diet" for mind, body, and spirit.

PRACTICE/MEDITATION

For today's practice, you will make a list of the foods you typically eat. What's different about this is that you will place those items in one of three categories.

To begin, get a sheet of paper and divide it into three columns. At the top of the left-hand column, write the heading, "Beneficial." In the center column, write the heading "Neither Beneficial Nor Harmful." In the right-hand column, write the heading "Harmful."

The idea here is to get a sense of whether your current diet is helping your mind, body and spirit or potentially hindering them. How do you know if a food should go in the "Beneficial" column? This column is for foods that are helping you achieve long-term health goals for body, mind and spirit.

The "Neither Beneficial Nor Harmful" category might be foods, for example, that are easy and convenient to eat, but are not necessarily the ideal choice. Neither are they the worst foods for you. They are adequate foods and useful for that purpose.

In the "Harmful" column are foods that might be okay to have from time to time, but they do not necessarily enhance your well-being and health goals.

The idea here is not to eat only the Beneficial foods, but to invite moderation and become more aware of your eating style and choices.

67

COMMUNITY

Serve Others After the Meal Is Over

The brothers should serve one another.
Consequently, no one will be excused from kitchen
service unless he is sick or engaged in some
important business of the monastery,
for such service increases reward and fosters love.
—Saint Benedict, *The Rule of St. Benedict*

Personally, I try to make a point of helping to clean up at mealtime. Even when I am a guest, I offer my assistance. That was not always the case, however. When I was in high school, I considered cleaning up a chore worthy only of extreme avoidance. Only now do I recognize the wisdom of parents who have their children assume responsibility around the kitchen or home. For example, the idea of taking responsibility is an integral part of the tea ceremony. The whole idea behind tea is to create mindfulness, harmony and respect between host and guest.

When we respect others we value them and take our share of the load. Introduce respect and responsibility as part of your family values and experience the change it creates.

PRACTICE/MEDITATION

For today's meal, take on a responsibility for part of the meal preparation or clean up as a way of showing respect and love for your family or community. Ideally, try doing something you haven't done in the past.

If roles for who does what in the kitchen are already established, try something new. Switch up those roles and responsibilities. Or, take on the chores of another so they can take a break. Don't be afraid to ask for help or get advice on how to best do the job.

After you have played a new role or taken on a responsibility as a guest, notice how that feels. By chipping in with your effort, you show respect and care for others. You have just entered the dynamic and heartwarming circle of giving and receiving. Marvelous!

68

EATING

Eat Like a Mindfulness Master

Mindfulness is free. We are born with it.
—Venerable U Silananda, Burmese monk and teacher

I still remember the morning I was told to sit opposite the head of the monastery during lunch. While this was an honor, I was mildly alarmed. What worried me was that U Silananda had written a well-known book about mindfulness. I was certain he would see my unsteady mind and mindless eating habits. But once I sat at the table, I decided to slow down and simply eat as if I already knew how to be mindful rather than be concerned about him watching me from across the table. It worked.

One of the things I appreciate most about mindfulness is that it is not only about our own eating. Mindfulness extends to those we are with. The monks I shared meals with always watched to see when someone needed more rice or food.

We, too, can be grateful and attentive to everything happening around us—even if we happen to be dining alone.

PRACTICE/MEDITATION

Today, you will eat your next meal as if you were already a mindfulness master. What does this mean? It means that you will harness your innate and very powerful capable power of attention. You needn't worry because as stated in the quote above, "Mindfulness is free. We are born with it." As a novice monk I was being interviewed by U. Silananda when he said those words to me. I remember being struck by the simplicity and truth of them. While we possess mindfulness, it only works if we apply it.

One way I like to describe this is that you can pour Ajax cleaner in a tub, but it won't clean the surface unless you scrub and use real elbow power!

Mindfulness is like Ajax. You already have it in your cupboard under the sink. Now, for this meal, use the effort and discipline of mindful awareness to scrub away the distractions, cravings and urges that often occur while eating.

When you chew, know that you are chewing. When you taste, know that you are tasting. When you swallow, know that you are swallowing. When the food travels down the esophagus, know that the food travels down the esophagus. When you take a breath or a pause, know that you take a breathe or a pause. When you notice that you are full and had enough, know that you are full and had enough.

Do this, and eat like the mindfulness master you already are!

69

COMMUNITY

Take the Hero's Journey with Food

*We need myths that will identify the individual
not with his local group but with the planet.*
—Joseph Campbell, *Myth and the Modern World*

Eating is not just about gulping down today's meal. There is a bigger picture to be found in the mythic journey of food. Myth is present in all life, and food is another mythic journey that we all travel. Discovering your universal journey regarding food may offer new insight into your life.

As a mythic food journeyer, you must answer a call—which might be anything from struggling with a diet to overcoming an illness. The movie *Star Wars*, for example, was tapped into the power of the mythic journey. When you decide to face and answer your call —as Luke Skywalker did in *Star Wars*—you, too, undergo trials and face fears that lead to greater knowledge and the dawning of wisdom. That is how you become a hero.

PRACTICE/MEDITATION

For this meditation, you will reflect on your journey with food and eating. What is the "call" that you are being asked to face or take? Maybe it's a call to find moderation in eating? Maybe it's a call to face the emotions and stresses that are driving unhealthy eating habits. Or, perhaps your journey is about becoming more open and less judgmental towards yourself and others.

I often explored the hero's journey with patients in the eating disorder clinic because it resonated with their own treatment journey. I remember a woman in her twenties who was about to be leave the program, but was very resistant to getting follow-up treatment and seeing an outside therapist for her recovery. After explaining the roadmap of the hero's journey—which included getting the call for treatment, leaving the ordinary world and entering the eating treatment world where the hero faces fears and learns new skills before returning home with new wisdom—this woman's hand shot up.

"Now I understand what I have to do!" she exclaimed. "To complete my journey I need to see a therapist so I can continue the journey and get ready for my next call."

Her recognition that the journey never really ends was a beautiful moment. While you alone take your hero's journey, always know that you have wise supporters who are with you and willing to help you. As you reflect on your call, take notes and keep digging deeper. Above all, we willing to take that next step into the healing unknown.

70

EATING

Say Yes to Life

In that first bite after my three-week fast,
I learned what all condemned prisoners,
downed pilots, and exiles know: that food is life,
and that eating is saying yes to life.
—Philip Zaleski & Paul Kaufman

At the other polarity of eating is fasting. Have you ever fasted or taken a break from food? Often, in many traditions, fasting and feasting are linked. Taking a break (or a brake) from eating, gives you a chance to appreciate food's value even more. And, it lets your digestive system rest.

If you are afraid to go without food for an extended period of time, there could be many reasons. These could include the experience of not having had enough food or deprivation. Thus, having food available at all times might make you feel safe and secure. These are normal feelings.

If you constantly eat and do not know why, remember that it is okay to take an occasional break from eating. In fact, you take a break from eating each night before you "break-fast" in the morning.

PRACTICE/MEDITATION

If having food close by makes you feel more secure, or if you have to completely clean off your plate because you worry about not getting enough—this practice will be helpful.

There are two parts to this meditation and practice. First, you will intentionally let go of food, even a little bit. You can achieve this in several ways. This could mean that you might consciously decide to stop snacking late at night or after your evening dinner. Or, you might set the intention of leaving some food on your plate at each meal—which acts as a sign that you are letting go of your worry about scarcity and lack of food. Another idea is to fast for part of the day. If you do decide to go without food for a period of time, allow yourself the flexibility to drink water, tea, or do what is necessary to maintain your health.

The second part of the practice is to joyfully appreciate your return to food. With that first bite and taste, savor the moment, knowing that you are saying "yes" to life. This is a huge affirmation that you can spread into other areas of your life. Each time you greet a family member, friend or colleague, savor the moment and know you are saying "yes" to life!

71

COMMUNITY

Feed Your Neighbor

. . . he asked Jesus, "And who is my neighbor?"
—Luke 10:29

When it comes to food and eating, who is your true neighbor? The Bible story of the Good Samaritan answers the question this way: A neighbor is one who is willing to offer food to someone—even a stranger—who is in distress or suffering. In real life, though, showing kindness to a stranger through food can be frightening.

I know a well-to-do family that enjoys every major convenience. Each year during Thanksgiving, however, the parents take their children to a homeless shelter where the whole family participates in feeding the homeless. One of the parents said, "I want our kids to know that there are people who have less and who need help." Can you show mercy and find your comfort zone at the same time?

Maybe you cannot. Still, you can face your fears and share food with your less fortunate neighbors when the opportunity arises.

PRACTICE/MEDITATION

This meditation is about the realization that you do not have to change the world. You can simply open your eyes and become less judgmental of those in need.

Have you ever turned away, or even felt repulsed by someone in need? I remember the time I lived in a beautiful beach town. But when I went to the grocery store one day, in the parking lot was an unkempt woman who commandeered a grocery cart filled with her belongings. I avoided her. But one day, I decided to talk with her. That's when I discovered she had once lived in this town as a resident. Unfortunately, poor health and financial difficulties caused a decline into homelessness. But this was still her town as much as it was mine. From that point on, I got to know her better, and I would buy her food whenever I saw her near the market.

It's easy to think that those who are struggling are different from us. But maybe they are just like us. As that old proverb says, "There but for the grace of God, go I."

To soften your heart, breathe in the words from the loving-kindness meditation, "May I be free from pain, hunger and suffering." Then, breathe out the words, "May all beings be free from pain, hunger and suffering." This recognizes that you and others are entwined. Let your compassion spread its wings as you breathe out and share the tender feelings of warmth and care you have for others.

72

EATING

Mindless Grazing and Food Portions

When we lose, I eat.
When we win, I eat.
I also eat when it's rained out.
—Tommy Lasorda

Are you someone who grazes on food constantly or is always looking for an eating opportunity? For some people, anytime is a good time to eat. But if you're mindlessly grazing, the first step to changing this or any fixed eating routine is becoming more aware of it.

The problem with grazing is that you may forget how often and how much you eat. It never seems like a large portion of food if you just eat a little bit at a time!

Another potential problem is that snack food can be filled with many calories but little nutritional value. Whether you graze when you are bored, lonely, happy, angry, upset, indifferent, playing video games or watching TV, increased awareness of your patterns is the first step to turning in a new direction.

PRACTICE/MEDITATION

For this practice you will do journaling. On a sheet of paper create three columns. Atop the left column write, "Time of Day." Atop the center column write, "Foods & Activities." The heading for the right column reads, "Types of Hunger." This sheet will help you recognize eating patterns and habits during the day. If possible, journal for a week to get a good snapshot of your food habits.

In the center column, itemize the foods you eat, as well as how much of each, and the activities you are engaged in while eating. Are you alone or with others? Are you on the computer? Describe activities *in detail*. Are you distracted by texting, watching a program, or using social media?

Finally, in the right hand column, rate your hunger. Is it physical or emotional? How strong is your hunger or craving—small, moderate or extreme? You can rate these using the 1-10 scale as was explained in Practice/Meditation #7.

Keep in mind that this practice requires moments of pause and reflection. This means slowing down, stopping, taking a breath. After journaling this information, take a few moments to reflect and digest what you are learning.

Do you notice any trends that contribute to mindless eating? Be kind to yourself and remember that this is not a time for blame or shame, just for open awareness. Finally, ask yourself: *Knowing what I know now, what is the best and kindest thing I could do for myself in this next moment?* Follow your own wise and mindful advice, whether it's stopping eating, having a fulfilling glass of water, changing activities or contacting a supportive friend.

73

COMMUNITY

All-You-Can-Eat Mindfulness Buffet

Next time you're in a buffet or cafeteria line,
notice how some people behave.
—Ronna Kabatznick, Ph.D., *The Zen of Eating*

Have you ever been to all-you-can-eat buffet? One exercise I often suggest to participants in my Mindful Eating workshops is to visit an all-you-can-eat buffet or fast food restaurant. I instruct them to pretend that they are visiting from another planet and have absolutely no idea what food or eating is all about. Their job is to just watch themselves and others (unobtrusively, of course) without judgment, craving, or opinion. As St. Francis of Assisi wrote in *A Simple Prayer*, "It is in forgiving that we are forgiven."

Often, eating taps into your fear of not getting enough food/abundance/health/success/love/protection, etc. And so, an all-you-can-eat buffet offers a kind of food security blanket. It seems to say, "you will be taken care of, you will have enough." And so the tendency is to eat as much as possible as a hedge against future scarcity and loss.

❧

PRACTICE/MEDITATION

For this practice, which is also a mindfulness meditation, you will be mindful of your judgments simply by noting them.

To begin, you can observe what is it like when you eat with others? Is your critical eating voice on overdrive? Do you wince when someone takes (or refuses) a large helping of dessert? Do you become judgmental when someone eats what you consider unhealthy, politically incorrect, ecologically unsound, or "fill in the blank"? Or, do you worry about others judging you?

You can quiet this critical voice just as Jesus did when he decided that compassion and forgiveness were more important than adhering to the traditional food codes practiced at the time. Basically, Jesus felt that criticism of how others ate created unholy judgments and distinctions between people sitting at the same table.

As you nurture feelings of compassion for how you (and others) eat, you can accept that there is no perfect way of eating. Besides, no one will eat the way you think is best—even if you know they'd benefit from healthier eating habits. For these same reasons, you do not need to judge yourself when you make a mistake.

74

EATING

Clear Mind, Calm Mind

To find the jewel, one must calm the waves;
it is hard to find if one stirs up the water.
—Mumon Yamada Roshi, Zen teacher

Does your mind resemble a murky pool at mealtime? Or is it filled with purpose and clarity? And, how can you tell the difference?

A murky mind is mired in confusion about what foods to eat. Such a mind critically judges the foods you (and others) eat. It could also be a mind filled with conflicting emotions about dieting and rules to follow.

If your mind is murky, do not fret. In Buddhist lore, the lotus represents the awakening consciousness of all beings. That's because it arises from muddy depths, yet reaches the surface clean and pristine. It turns out the lotus possesses a special property. It's superhydrophobic, which means nothing sticks to it!

Fortunately, like the lotus, our mind can be cleansed until it blossoms into the jewel of clear consciousness. And that means greater food clarity.

PRACTICE/MEDITATION

For this meditation, you will use a single word or words to focus on as you eat your meal. Since this is best accomplished by not speaking, it's best to have this meal alone, where you can focus on your meal and your calming word(s).

Meditative practices have long used mantras, or sacred words and phrases, to help focus attention and increase concentration. The right words can also prime us for feelings of calm, closeness, and compassion.

The idea here is to find a word that will center and calm your mind during the meal. What word or phrase is meaningful to you? What word envelops you in a soft and warm light?

Here are a few ideas to consider: Peace, Father, Mother, Love, God, Jesus, Buddha, One, Shalom, Om, Calm, Mindfully Eating, Just This, or any other words that come to mind can work, even if it's the name of someone who you have loved.

As you sit down to eat, set the intention to have your chosen word help you to eat mindfully and for the whole health of your mind, body and spirit. It's important that you do not force the word. Just imagine it whispering like the wind. If it disappears or your mind wanders, that's okay. Just gently come back to your calming word. Place about half your attention on the word and about half on the eating, chewing, tasting and body movement as you eat. How marvelous!

75

COMMUNITY

Necessary and Essential Blessings

From my own personal experience I can tell you
that when I practice altruism and care for others,
it immediately makes me calmer and more secure.
—The Dalai Lama, *Transforming the Mind*

No matter how challenging your personal eating or dieting issues are, you are not alone in your pain. And, even if you are at a state of relative peace with your eating, there are ways to lessen the pain of others.

In some traditions, the idea of offering help to others is not voluntary, but necessary and essential. The Jewish practice of *mitzvah*, or doing good deeds, is a means by which service to others is commanded by God. Feeding the hungry, inviting others to dinner, and giving charity to the homeless are important ways of sharing kindness and showing that you care.

Mitzvah, or any good deed, is not a burden but a personal bless-ing. It is a blessing to know that by feeding others you can make a difference. This is empowerment, too, because you help others to sustain themselves and grow as a result.

PRACTICE/MEDITATION

What is the special blessing related to food that you could share? Is there a mitzvah hiding in plain sight for you to discover and reveal to others?

For this practice, you can reflect on something you can offer to the community. Think of this as a personal mitzvah or good deed that you have the privilege of offering. To make this more interesting, consider a group mitzvah.

With your children, partner, friend, work associates or other group, cook up an idea for doing a good deed that relates to food. It could mean collecting canned goods for distribution, volunteering at a food bank, or raising money for a food drive.

Get curious and look around, and you will find the necessary and essential blessing with your name on it.

STEP 4
DEPARTURE

Departure completes your 4-Step Food Journey. But don't be fooled into thinking that this step is just about exiting the meal. Here, you'll learn to let go fully, as you digest the moment and move forward with a sense of peace, fulfillment and acceptance for all this meal has given you. *How you depart* can leave you with a lingering last taste that prepares you for continuing your journey with humility, grace and wonder.

76

DEPARTURE

Mealtime Peace and Acceptance

May peace be with you.
—Mount Calvary Monastery, Santa Barbara, CA

Traditionally, Benedictine monks practice eight "Canonical Hours of the Divine Office," or periods of prayer throughout the day. When I attended such prayers during a visit to Mount Calvary Monastery, each session ended in the same way. We walked the room greeting each person face-to-face and said, "May peace be with you," before heading out for the rest of the day. It is hard, if not impossible, to be angry or hold a grudge when departing with such heartfelt and tender thoughts in one's heart and mind!

As one meal ends, another journey begins. How can you depart your meal in the same way those prayer sessions ended—holding on to a sense of peace, tenderness and warmth?

PRACTICE/MEDITATION

For today's meditation, you will reflect on how to be at peace with the meal you have just eaten. Much of this has to do with full acceptance of your meal experience.

Acceptance can be thought of as nonresistance. When you really think about it, it's where we resist the reality of the moment that causes suffering. For example, blaming yourself or feeling guilty about what foods you eat or how much you eat means you're pushing against what has already happened. Blaming yourself for past actions doesn't change a thing. Looking in the rear view mirror blocks you from having a clear view of the present moment.

It might help to remember that you eat thousands of meals in a lifetime. *There is no one perfect meal for you.* With this awareness, see what it's like *not to resist* your choices. By not resisting, you are less constricted and tight.

Take a nice breath and set the intention to accept yourself eating style and food choices for this meal. Exhale with a long, slow breathe . . . AHHHhhhh. This is the AHHHhhhh of acceptance, the AHHH-hhhh of letting go demands. It is the AHHHhhhh of peace and tenderness. Take one of these breaths anytime during the meal that you feel yourself holding on or resisting.

As you prepare to leave your meal, check in on what energy fills your body. Are you drowsy? Alert? Anxious? Guilty? Regretful? Accept whatever is present, knowing that you can make different choices at your next meal. With full acceptance, may you find peace after today's meal!

77

DEPARTURE

What's Eating You After Eating?

When the pain of loneliness comes upon you,
confront it, look at it without
any thought of running away.
—Krishnamurti, *Think On These Things*

For some, food can be used to evade or distract from difficult emotions. I can recall a time in my own life, shortly after graduating from college, when I ate comfort food (rice pudding) to ease the pain of loneliness. Unfortunately, as soon as I finished eating, I was alone again with my thoughts and my loneliness.

You may adopt a strict diet plan as a way to ignore uncomfortable feelings about your emotions or body. But pushing your feelings underground only lets them hide in wait, where the feelings will ambush you by causing you to lose control of that diet. Better to give feelings a voice and make friends with these difficult emotions. In the long run, this is how to heal food cravings.

PRACTICE/MEDITATION

For this practice, you will investigate the emotions you feel both during and after you leave your meal. That's really the essence of the saying, "It's not what you're eating, it's what's eating you." This is not as scary as it might seem, because mindfulness isn't about having to change anything, but a way to recognize deeper truth and embody your whole being.

If you're upset while eating, know that you're upset. See the truth about *what* and *how* you eat affect your mood. A meal eaten in haste and anxiety can naturally cause you to carry those feelings with you after leaving the table. If you are dissatisfied or unhappy after your meal, for example, do you ever take that feeling with you —to your next meeting or environment?

It can be helpful to just feel the sensations and name the emotions you are experiencing. Find as many emotions as are present. For example, anger is often an offshoot of hurt. Sadness may also contain feelings of disappointment or dismay. You don't have to change these feelings, avoid them or replace them. Simply be present with them as part of the *whole you*. After all, the ancient word for mindfulness, *sati*, means self-remembrance and self-recollecting. It's about bringing the fragmented and lost parts of yourself together. That's your innate wholeness—a living, breathing, emotional, conscious being—that evolved with the Universe over a period of 13 billion years. How fabulous!

78

DEPARTURE

Forget the Nonessentials

Throw out nonessential numbers.
This includes age, weight and height.
Let the doctor worry about them.
That is why you pay him/her.
—George Carlin, comedian

What nonessential numbers do you carry with you throughout the day? Do you constantly weigh yourself? Do you measure your calories and count your victories (and losses) at each meal? True, some numbers can be important—like blood pressure, blood sugar level, etc. But some, however, are just ways to occupy your mind and time.

One of the keys to skillful departure from mealtime is a willingness to be open to the unknown. What would happen, for example, if you did not weigh yourself for a day or two?

Openness does not mean you are uncertain, undecided and lost. It means that you are willing to let each day unfold freely and with a sense of wonder, rather than following a predetermined script or computer program as a machine might do. This is the kind of unknowing that lets you fully inhabit the present moment.

PRACTICE/MEDITATION

For this practice, you will consciously decide to enter a period of openness, unknowing and freedom after mealtime.

First, think about your typical after-meal routine. Do you weigh yourself? Do you jump on the computer or some other device? Do you start working immediately? Do you spend any time reflecting?

You can also inquire: When did this particular routine first begin? Is it satisfying? What keeps this routine in place? What are the consequences physical, emotional or spiritual consequences of this habit for you?

Old routines might have been useful, but for the sake of this practice, you will intentionally try a new path.

What new activities or behaviors would take you into the space of unknowing and openness after today's meal? The options are endless, really. Even if your time is limited, you can experience a lot in just five minutes time.

If you're outside, you could watch for unusual birds, plants, flowers, cloud shapes and trees. Open yourself to the natural world with a childlike presence and curiosity. Or, you might have a conversation with someone new or read something meaningful and inspiring for five minutes. And, there's always the option of focusing on your breath or just "being" for a few minutes.

79

DEPARTURE

Acceptance and Compassion for Dessert

True acceptance is saying, "It's all right,
it's all right, it's all right."
—Emmanuel, *Emmanuel's Book*

Have you ever eaten at birthday, wedding or other celebration where food was plentiful? Chances are that either you or someone you know has been tempted to eat more than normal. When this happens, how accepting are you of your actions?

Have you ever said to yourself, "That proves I can't control my eating," or "I have zero willpower and can't stay on a diet?" At times like this you need to remember that this is only one meal and no crime has been committed!

Acceptance is like a salve that heals those self-inflicted wounds. It gives you kindness and compassion when you can find none. Is there anyone who has not struggled with eating at one time or another? All physical beings struggle for and with food. Only you can forgive the unforgiving voice within.

PRACTICE/MEDITATION

Acceptance is one of those life practices that takes time and is best experienced in multiple ways. If acceptance is something that resonates with you, then you might want to review practice #76, which explores the power acceptance.

Today's practice pairs acceptance with its natural companion, compassion. Acceptance helps us release the negative thoughts and feelings we may have around eating. Compassion is emotive, because it softens our view and supports us in time of emotional upheaval. When you break down the word *com-passion*, it means "to be with-suffering." So, when you have compassion for another or for yourself, you help carry the burden of suffering. When you think about it, compassion is a step beyond empathy—where you feel and understand another's pain.

Compassion means you have the impulse to *step in and act* in a way that lightens the burden of suffering. It's a beautiful human act, and it is something that defines who we are as conscious, human beings.

Sit with the meaning of compassion as you eat today's meal. How can you bring compassion to yourself in this moment? What kind thought or action would lessen the unique burden that you may be carrying?

Right now, rest with compassion and acceptance, and forgive yourself for meals eaten mindlessly.

80

DEPARTURE

Don't Waste Time on the Waist

The Master gives himself up
to whatever the moment brings.
—Lao Tzu

D o you frequently worry about your waistline? Do you compare your adult body shape to the body shape you had in your teens or twenties? Syndicated columnist Dave Barry once wrote, "A waist is a terrible thing to mind." But by constantly checking your weight or waistline, you are defining yourself in a very limited way. You cannot measure who you are as a whole person by simple numbers.

I am not saying that you should not try to look and feel your best. But how realistic are your expectations? What weight and body standards do you hold yourself up to? Do your expectations make you feel angry, disappointed, frustrated with yourself and your body?

The truth is this: Your body ages and changes. This is a natural process for all persons—and for all living things. To surrender to our fragility and accept this truth is to appreciate the preciousness of the moment.

PRACTICE/MEDITATION

This meditation focuses on being aware of negative feelings toward your body, as well as emotionally honoring your body.

Having worked in an eating disorder clinic, I learned firsthand how media images and portrayals of female bodies affected the mindset of young women. Research has shown that media is a factor in causing low self-esteem, depression and other emotional issues. Today, with the advent of artificial intelligence, body shapes and faces can be manipulated more easily than ever before. That's why it's important to be mindful of the bodies and images that you watch on social media, TV, magazines, advertisements, and so on. Do these truly represent what is out there in the real world? How do they affect you?

Here's the practice: Today, you will attempt to catch or notice all the thoughts and feelings you have about your body. This is no easy task! You'll have to be diligent. That's because screen images tend to quickly hijack your attention—taking it away from inner reflection.

What kinds of habits and thought patterns do body centered images stimulate in your mind? It might help to keep a record of these on a pad of paper or on your phone.

You can also invoke a sense of caring and appreciation for your own body. Throughout the day, notice all it does for you on a daily basis! This is truly miraculous and worthy of gratitude.

81

DEPARTURE

Laughter Solution and Soul-ution

*Hearty laughter is a good way to jog
internally without having to go outdoors.*
—Norman Cousins, author

What is your mood after eating? Do you get anxious that you ate too much (little)? Do you feel heavy and weighted down because of what you ate? Do you go right from eating to intense physical or mental activity? If you experience pronounced moods or feelings such as these, then you could benefit from a gentler mealtime transition.

A skillful departure is essential to experiencing emotional joy and balance with eating. Eating is a time of enjoyment, so why not (en)lighten your departure with a transition of laughter and bliss? To begin, here's a lighthearted quote from comedienne Totie Fields, who said, "I've been on a diet for two weeks and all I've lost is two weeks."

PRACTICE/MEDITATION

Today's practice strives to create a lighter and brighter transition out of today's meal. But first, let's address that tendency to weigh oneself after eating. If that's part of an after meal routine, consider doing the unthinkable—give that scale away or put it in your closet or out of view, at least for the moment.

To brighten your mealtime departure you can purposely seek out something positive or humorous. Even noticing all the pleasant things around you in the present moment—clouds in the sky, children playing, a rose bush, fresh air, your own sense of aliveness—can enhance your sense of happiness and well-being.

You might consider having pleasant conversation with another, reading a few engaging pages in a favorite book, or enjoying a fragrant cup of tea. You could make the executive decision to text or call that one special person who always seems to make you laugh or smile. Or, you could practice being G.L.A.D. as explored in Practice/Meditation #63.

How does a more uplifting transition make you feel after eating? By selectively focusing on the positive, you can alter how you feel in the present moment. How empowering!

82

DEPARTURE

The Secret of Letting Go

There is a time for departure,
even when there's no certain place to go.
—Tennessee Williams

D o you ever find it difficult to bid farewell after a meal? Do you hold on to mealtime sights, sounds, and tastes? Do you constantly replay dinner conversation or wish that you had eaten differently? If so, you might appreciate the February 4th farewell celebration for the Chinese kitchen god. This is when many Chinese leave offerings of salty fish or sticky sweet cakes for a kitchen god who returns to heaven to report on each family's behavior. A good report results in bountiful cupboards in the year to come.

If you were a kitchen god, what report would you make about your mealtime farewell behavior? It is normal to remember mealtime events. But a mindful departure means being present here and now.

This lets you exit gracefully and not overstay your welcome. Staying is easy. Leaving is an art.

PRACTICE/MEDITATION

For this practice, you will observe how you hold on after departing your meal. Each time you find yourself holding on to that past meal, take a breath, relax and gently let go.

When we are mentally or physically attached to anything, we tend to grab on tightly. This reminds me the story I heard about of how hunters captured monkeys by hollowing out a gourd that was fixed to the ground. The gourd had a hole just large enough for a monkey's hand to fit through and grab the tempting food that was placed inside. This was an ingenious trap because once the monkey grasped the food with a clenched fist, its hand was too big to pull out.

Yes, the monkey could escape by relaxing and releasing the food. But the iron grip of attachment, greed and desire kept it stuck. The monkey was trapped simply by its own unwillingness to let go!

Use this powerful metaphor anytime you are caught in magnetic pull of the past. The trick is to become aware of trap—which is mind traveling to the past. When this happens, give yourself permission to take a breath and let go. When you feel the in-breath and out-breath you have escaped the trap and returned to the present moment.

Rest in the here and now after that last meal. It's a wonderful place to be.

83
DEPARTURE

The Mindful Walking Departure

If we live in mindfulness, we are no longer poor,
because our practice of living in the present moment
makes us rich in joy, peace, understanding, and love.
—Thich Nhat Hanh, *Our Appointment With Life*

One positive way to experience mindfulness after mealtime is to take a walk. This is an ancient prescription for health. The Buddha, for example, recommended this over 2,500 years ago. The Greek doctor Hippocrates also recommended exercise for long life. Of course, this is contrary to the words of a comedian who once commented, "every time I feel the urge to exercise, I lie down."

The choice is yours, but once you try mindful walking you may decide to make it more of a healthy habit after eating. While some mindful walking is done slowly, you can also walk quickly or briskly if that fits your style.

PRACTICE/MEDITATION

Today, you will engage in an intentional mindful walking method to get present and invigorated after your meal. It uses three basic principles that are detailed below: 1) Setting an Intention, 2) Following Up with Action, and 3) Observation.

How long you want to walk is up to you, but even a short walk can be beneficial. In fact, anytime you want to interrupt an addictive pattern, anxious thinking or an old habit, a short mindful walk will refocus your attention on the body's moment-by-moment movement. And, the same basic three steps can be applied whether walking, sitting, cooking or eating. To start your walking practice, find a quiet place where you won't be interrupted, either indoors or outdoors. Then, follow the steps below:

1) *Setting the Intention* to take a step with your left foot.

2) *Following Up with Action* by taking the step.

3) *Observation* means paying attention to all the sensations that occur as your foot raises up, moves forward, and sets down on the ground. Notice how your knee bends, how your heel touches the ground, and how your weight shifts from one side of the body to the other as you set down your foot.

4) Repeat steps 1-3 for the other foot, leg, or when turning.

Just breathe normally as you walk. Since this might slow you down, your balance could be compromised. It can help to stand beside a wall so you can steady yourself. Or, just speed up the pace and walk more briskly, just noticing each step and movement and thinking to yourself, "walking, walking." If your mind wanders, gently bring your attention back to the your next intention.

84

DEPARTURE

Discover Your After Meal Rhythm

I do not think that anything serious should be done
after dinner, as nothing should be before breakfast.
—George Saintsbury, 20th century British critic

How can you make a graceful transition from mealtime? How can you settle yourself down, without the pressure to immediately jump back on life's treadmill?

In many countries it is common to take a break or siesta after lunch. Why is this? That is probably because the body is busy digesting the meal. Drowsiness is one reason, for example, why a sitting meditating after eating a meal can be difficult.

It can be hard to think on a full stomach since the blood rushes from the head to the stomach to digest the meal. And so, you need to recognize how digestion alters your body and mind.

PRACTICE/MEDITATION

For this practice, you will seek peace after mealtime. How can you make space before transitioning to a period of activity or generativity?

Here are a few ideas. If a siesta is not accepted at your workplace, find a few moments of solitude where you can close your eyes. Or, take a short, calming nature walk—or an intentional mindful walk as explained in practice #83. Walking always makes for a good transition, as well as aiding in digestion.

Another idea? Find a calming or soothing object that you can savor for a few moments. This can be anything from looking at favorite photos and playing music to holding a treasured object or watching the natural world.

Pausing with an after meal cup of tea is also ideal as an after meal transition. This simple ritual signifies closure and helps stifle continuous snacking or eating because it sends the clear message that the meal is over; it's time to move on to what's next.

If you are still not feeling ready to undertake tasks that demand more energy and brain power, you might want to try Practice/Meditation #93, *Your Portable and Refreshing After Meal Mint*, which engages deep breathing as a tool to build up energy after eating, as well as anytime you feel sluggish.

85

DEPARTURE

Fidelity to Cleaning Up

Relying on yourself to do the little things—
like cleaning up carefully after the meal,
doing chores gracefully and mindfully,
not banging kettles—helps develop
concentration and makes practice easier.
—Achaan Chah, Buddhist monk

Do you clean up quietly and mindfully after a meal? Do you sweep the floor with grace? Or, do you leave the kitchen untended and the sink full of dishes?

Saint Benedict was a 6th century Italian monk whose *Rule of Saint Benedict* laid out guidelines for those on a spiritual path. To that end, novice monks were instructed to take a vow of *conversatio morum*, which translates as "fidelity to monastic life." But the word *conversatio* means a "conversion of life," and in this sense it holds a deeper meaning. In their book *Contentment*, authors Robert Johnson and Jerry Ruhl consider this to mean "a vow of fidelity to the moment." How beautiful a concept for helping us go off auto-pilot and consciously clean up after a meal.

PRACTICE/MEDITATION

Anyone can use the concept of fidelity to the moment as a modern means of clearing out clutter or cleaning up after a meal.

With fidelity to the moment, you contact that dish, that person, that morsel in a direct and fresh way—instead of just having the mind jump in and label it as "oh, there's another chore or dish to clean."

With fidelity to the moment, there is no right or wrong way to approach cleanup. There is only experiencing fully the way you leave your kitchen after eating. Whatever you do, see if you can be faithful to each task, giving it your full attention. Should you place the dishes in the sink for washing later, place them thoughtfully. Use this cleaning moment to slow your actions and your thoughts down.

Mindful cleaning will do more than reduce the possibility of broken dishes and accidents. In the long run, it offers compassion toward oneself. If you have not used fidelity to the moment as a style of cleaning, give it a try. Remember, too, that you can enjoy fidelity to the breath and fidelity to others as you share the cleaning up moment.

86

DEPARTURE

Ultimate Non-Clinging Lesson

*An integral being knows without going, sees
without looking, and accomplishes without doing.*
—Lao Tzu, Chinese Taoist Philosopher

It has been said that the Buddha's teachings could be condensed and distilled down to basically one core idea: "Cling to nothing whatsoever." Of course, that's easier said than done. You could say that humans are a study in getting attached and staying attached—to people, objects, ideas, beliefs, and emotions, to name just a few.

Suppose, for example, that a dinner trip to your favorite restaurant leaves you feeling highly disappointed. Do you quickly let go of your negative emotions and enjoy what's left of your evening? Or, do you stubbornly carry last meal's badly prepared fish, poor customer service or thoughtless presentation with you long afterwards? Doing the latter could result in negative, undigested emotions—not to mention a possible case of indigestion. Fortunately, you can leave your mealtime disappointments behind by practicing mindful equanimity. Don't underestimate the power of equanimity. It is one of Buddhism's *Brahamaviharas*, or divine abodes—states of mind and being that enlightened ones strive for.

PRACTICE/MEDITATION

For this practice, you will use mindfulness and equanimity to move past grasping and clinging. How does equanimity play a role in food and eating? Equanimity means you take mealtime highs and lows with the same attitude of peace and calm. Think of equanimity as a still and calm water at the bottom of the ocean. It is unaffected by the storms and waves at the surface.

In the same way, equanimity allows for a calm, spacious state of mind that does not cling to past mealtime events. This means it doesn't matter whether the restaurant food was fabulous or horrendous, whether the service was the best or worst ever, you are immune to the highs and lows because you are clinging to none of them. (Naturally, this doesn't mean you'll forget and return for another bad meal!)

To cultivate equanimity, use each breath to let go of the negative emotions—that cling to you like super glue. Sit or stand as you breathe slowly, into your belly. Take a few breaths, and then scan your body to feel for the tension, emotion or attachment point.

Once you locate this, inhale deeply, imagining the air filling the area with healing relaxation and coolness. Visualize the breath dissolving the glue, and let each exhale wash the glue of negativity and tension from your mind, body and spirit. Use this cleansing and purifying breath whenever you notice that you are losing equanimity and calm.

87

DEPARTURE

Transitioning Between Meals

Change can happen at any time,
but transition comes along when one chapter
of your life is over and another is
waiting in the wings to make its entrance.
—William Bridges, *The Way of Transition*

According to change expert and author William Bridges, change is simply a situational shift. It is during the transition where we do all the work. Transition as he describes it has three distinct steps, or aspects:

Letting Go can be difficult. Each time you commit to new foods, for example, you must say goodbye to the old ones that are being replaced.

The Neutral Zone represents chaos and uncertainty. This is the time when you do not know what will happen next.

Beginning Again raises the question of how to adapt to the new "chapter" of eating, diet, and foods?

In terms of eating, that means the space between your last meal and your next one encompasses all three of these elements. That's a lot of change and transitioning!

PRACTICE/MEDITATION

What kinds of food transitions are you experiencing right now? Periods of transition can raise anxiety and put the brain's ancient alarm system on high alert.

Several practices in *Simply Mindful Meal by Meal* examine the process calming and letting go. But when you're between meals and in the *Neutral Zone*, you may have to tolerate a period without food or eating.

There is no magic pill to move through transitions. But mindfulness can shine the light of awareness on what's happening in the moment. You can recognize, for example, that you are in the *Neutral Zone*. Or, that your body needs some quick nutrition.

It's worth mentioning that getting some protein every two to three hours is critical to the optimal functioning of the decision-making part of the brain. Proteins are broken down into amino acids that are the building blocks for your brain's neurotransmitters. So having some cheese, nuts, or hard boiled eggs—foods that are easy to store and portable—might help.

88

DEPARTURE

Appreciate Your Biological Systems

*Without an efficient system of waste removal
we would rapidly poison ourselves;
moreover, as any gardener or farmer knows,
the products of elimination nourish the earth.*
—Philip Zaleski & Paul Kaufman

E ach time you eat food, as well as eliminate food waste from your body, you witness the miraculous workings of a biological system developed over thousands of years. Your body absorbs food's energy to create new cells and regenerate the body. It eliminates the rest.

This process is extremely complex, but your body manages it with amazing efficiency. Yet, this part of your body's operation is often ignored or not openly talked about. Elimination is a signal of how well your body is working. Regular or irregular bowel movements can tell a lot about your inner health and well-being. So, too, can intestinal problems such as irritable bowel syndrome and colitis. I have one friend, for example, who takes two capsules of liquid garlic after dinner to promote elimination and a healthy colon.

PRACTICE/MEDITATION

Take some time after meal to reflect on your body's elimination process. Be thankful for it as part of your sacred process of being.

It may also help to inquire how you mentally view the elimination process. The fact that it is often joked about or not openly expressed, tells us something about our societal and cultural views. What would it be like to bring this part of your body's life out of the shadows, without shaming or shunning a natural process of life?

One way to begin can be to appreciate or get curious at how your body absorbs and eliminates what it needs for well-being. While much of this is done in the background, how can you heed your body's signals when there is discomfort or imbalance of any kind?

As with eating, it is possible to be present with the elimination process by just noticing and paying attention. With mindfulness, you can be fully present, neither grasping for nor avoiding and pushing away each experience.

89

DEPARTURE

Take Stock of Your Own Harvest

Over the winter glaciers,
I see the summer glow,
And through the wild-piled snowdrift
The warm rose buds below.
—Ralph Waldo Emerson

Earlier, you've explored the seasonal needs of the body (#17) and seasonal shifts relating to springtime and preparation (#50). If you have already experienced many of the exercises in this book, then now may be a good time for harvesting, gathering and assessing the fruits of your labor—tasks that mark the autumnal equinox.

Do you bring harmony and balance to your body after eating? Do you listen to your body closely? Or, do you continue to eat and nibble even though you are no longer hungry? In the winter, a farmer must wait until the thaw before knowing what seeds to plant. For you, the "thaw" must be felt in your body.

PRACTICE/MEDITATION

For today's practice, you will bring awareness to your body in order to harvest harmony and acknowledge the fruits of your effort and discipline thus far.

After today's meal and cleanup, find a quiet place to transition. As you sit in a chair, take a mindful breath. Notice the in-breath and out-breath. Now, starting from the bottom of the feet and working your way up to the top of your head, you will use your awareness to scan your body. Do this like an impartial witness who is just observing.

Placing your attention on your feet, feel how they touch the ground. Do they feel bloated, fatigued, tense, or at ease? Notice whatever sensations arise. Don't hold onto any feeling; simply notice and release each. In this way, you make space for the next sensation, and the next.

If a sensation is pleasant, you don't need to hold onto it. Or, if a sensation is unpleasant, you don't need to push it away. Just notice each in a neutral way—just as you might notice a color as red, green, or blue. A color is not innately a good or bad. It's just that color! Likewise, a sensation in your body is not innately good or bad. It's just that sensation.

Continue to slowly scan your calves, thighs, hips, inner organs, torso, hands, arms, shoulders, neck, face, head and skull.

Take heart in the harvest of mindfulness you have brought into your life. What new seeds and mindful attitudes did you cultivate throughout this past season? Congratulate yourself on your food journey!

90

DEPARTURE

Break Free from Comparisons

*It often happens that I awake at night and begin
to think about a serious problem and decide I
must tell the pope about it. Then I wake up
completely and remember that I am the pope.*
—Pope John XXIII

What would it be like if you stopped to realize, as did Pope John XXIII, that maybe *you* are that most important person in your life, the wise one in charge who possesses all the answers?!

Since that's not always easy, we may end up comparing ourselves with others and saying things like: "I'm eating healthier (worse) than (fill in the blank) is." "Why don't I have willpower like (fill in the blank)?" Or, "How can (fill in the blank) eat those foods and not gain an ounce of weight?"

True, there is a lot of food wisdom and guidance to be gained from nutritionists, friends, therapists, family members, doctors, and so on. However, only you can realize that eating is not a competition or comparison. To let go of judgment is to grow in self-acceptance.

❦

PRACTICE/MEDITATION

For this practice you will let go of measuring your eating habits against others. The Buddha once said—as written in the *Dhamma-pada*, a book of his teachings:

> *The winner sows hatred*
> *Because the loser suffers.*
> *Let go of winning and losing*
> *And find joy.*

Without comparison there is no winner, no loser, no striving to change or fight against the way things happen to be. Instead, there is the simple acceptance of your eating and tolerance of others' eating. By subtracting the judgment, comparison and measuring, all that remains is mindfulness: this food, this eating, chewing and swallowing, and you receiving nourishment.

You are the master of your life and you determine—through your effort and skill and commitment—how you will use food. Ultimately, whether you use food for health, pleasure, medication, control, or love is your decision. Just watch. Be mindful of your emotions.

Then, like the pope, you can wake up and know that you possess everything it takes to start doing what needs to be done right now. How phenomenal!

91

DEPARTURE

Find What Is Pleasant

The lunches of fifty-seven years had caused
his chest to slip down to the mezzanine floor.
—P.G. Wodehouse

D o you feel like your body has shifted in new directions after you eat—maybe even toward the mezzanine? Or do you feel light, awake, and invigorated? It pays to take notice of this at your mealtime departure.

What does it feel like to eat a little less (or more) than you are used to eating? Do you feel uncomfortable or unsatisfied? Departure time is a good time to notice how much you actually need to feel full.

Also, take time to sense how *fulfilling* the meal has been to you at this time. If you do not in the least feel physically and mentally satisfied, then maybe a change of diet is in order.

PRACTICE/MEDITATION

For this practice, you will tune into your body after mealtime and note how satisfied you feel.

Let's take a moment to explain satisfaction. Satisfaction is more than a feeling of being physically "full." You might eat an entire cake at one sitting and feel full, but you probably won't feel very satisfied with the level of nourishment or how it makes you feel an hour later.

Satisfaction is different because it's a sensation that attends to your whole being—the biological, mental, social and spiritual aspects of who you are. This can be a pleasant and contented feeling. It might be a feeling deep in your cells, telling you that this meal in its entirety left you feeling uplifted, fulfilled and contented. A meal that accomplishes this usually comprises not only the food, but all of the surroundings and the people involved.

It's important that you remember the distinction between the kind of satiety that is merely physical and the deeper satisfaction that fulfills and uplifts all parts of you. I'm not saying that every meal must resonate with your social, emotional and spiritual selves. But knowing the ingredients for such a meal is vital.

If a meal doesn't quite have all the elements to make it deeply satisfying, you are always at liberty to spice it up *after* the meal.

Take a stroll. Sit outside for a moment to admire nature's splendor. Have a pleasant conversation with someone. Share a text or note about your meal with another. Find something pleasant in your life or surroundings at this very moment that brings you joy.

92

DEPARTURE

Charge Up Your Battery

*With each inhalation, your body takes in tens of
billions of atoms, tiny fragments of the universe
that over the centuries have passed through countless
numbers of other living beings and will continue
to do so long after you are no longer here.*
—Deepak Chopra, *Overcoming Addiction*

At the most basic level, food passes through you, charging you up like a battery. Then, it is gone, without a trace, miraculously being transformed into cells in your body.

As you depart your meal, know that food is doing what it is supposed to do. Its primary purpose is, after all, to nourish you. It is not an enemy whose purpose is to make you grow fat, unattractive and undesirable. Neither is it a confidante who will make you pretty, handsome and svelte.

If you emphasize choices that enhance the nourishment and well-being of your energy body, then you can let the meal go. But if your emotions are tied into how your body looks, then letting go may be more difficult.

PRACTICE/MEDITATION

For this meditation, you will set the intention to choose to leave food emotions and body image concerns behind after eating.

If you read the previous sentence and thought, "No way can I just leave it behind," that's okay. In terms of brain science, changing habits can feel impossible because when brain connections are frequently used and exercised, they become hard-wired. That's why entrenched habits, such as looking in the mirror after a meal, or even "body checking" and pinching your waist to see if you've gained weight, take time to change.

Setting your intention to do something different creates new links and wiring in the brain. This is how you, as a conscious choice-maker, can break the old habit right now.

Will the hard-wiring of the behavior still be there? Yes, but over time it can be replaced by a more helpful and choice driven behavior.

Remember, you make thousands and thousands of lifetime choices. By intentionally letting go of old emotional patterns and behaviors, you create space for new actions that could change your day—and life—in surprising ways.

93

DEPARTURE

Enjoy a Refreshing After-Meal Mint

I'm the paragon of a couch potato.
I've got six couches.
—Chef Bill Wavrin

Even professional chefs can have problems with their weight. Chef Bill Wavrin, for example, had problems moderating his eating due to sluggishness. Do you ever struggle with this same issue?

Sleepiness, sluggishness, or laziness right after leaving a meal can be a normal thing. But if it turns into three hours of mindlessly eating junk food on the couch or at the video console, then you need to stop the pattern and energize yourself.

In addition, maintaining energy after eating can be difficult due to cultural norms and schedules—such as following a rigid 3-meal-a-day routine. When enforced cultural habits hijack your body's natural rhythms, you may want to re-examine these. Today, with more people working from home, it does not make sense to force yourself to eat before your body signals you that the time is right.

PRACTICE/MEDITATION

What follows is a practice that I often used to overcome sluggishness after lunch when presenting workshops. In just a couple of minutes, it can boost your energy level. First, however, make sure you are eating at times that follow your body's natural rhythms. Consider the advice of Zen Master Rinzai, who said, "When hungry I eat; when tired, I sleep. Fools laugh at me. The wise understand."

Sit in a chair with your back straight. Now take a deep breath by inhaling deep into your diaphragm. To do this, you first want to relax the abdominal muscles. When you're ready, take a long in-breath for 6-8 counts. If you breathe into the lower part of the lungs, the lungs in turn will press down on the abdominal cavity. This is why the stomach moves outwards when breathing in.

Once you notice the stomach moving out, hold your breath for another 6-8 seconds. Then, very slowly release the breath through the mouth. Take at least five breaths like this. This practice will build up heat and energy in your body. Do it until you feel a surge of alertness.

You might think of this deep breathing practice as an after-meal breath mint that quickly refreshes you. In fact, anytime you feel tired during the day, you can quickly re-energize yourself using this deep breath practice.

94

DEPARTURE

Freedom of Forgiveness

*The more one lets go, the stronger the presence
of the Spirit becomes. The Ultimate Mystery
becomes the Ultimate Presence.*
—Father Thomas Keating

L etting go of mealtime emotions can require forgiveness for oneself. After all, who is to blame for your eating issues? Do you blame your parents, your caregivers, and others for saddling you with eating problems? Yes, you may be absolutely correct that they had a role in it—but now, as an adult, you need to do something for yourself. You might want the person whose behavior harmed you to suffer, but will that help your eating issue?

Forgiving does not mean forgetting. But it does mean that you are ready to move beyond your hurt and your pain and to start living in the present again. This is something you can do for your own well-being.

PRACTICE/MEDITATION

To begin this forgiveness reflection, find a place that helps you feel safe and at peace. Think about someone (alive or passed on) who always held your best interests in their heart. Imagine this person nearby, supporting you.

Next, let's reflect on the inherent fragility and frailty of human beings. There is not a single person alive who hasn't been harmed in some way. Everyone who lives long enough will suffer from old age and lose someone close to them. What if all of these suffering humans held a grudge?

To forgive is difficult. But to not forgive means locking yourself in a jail cell of anger, hurt and righteousness. Fortunately, you can unlock your cell and get yourself free.

Holding a warm wish in your heart for the well-being of others is incompatible with feelings of anger and retribution. The ancient loving-kindness practice—which engenders love and kindness for all beings— begins with forgiveness:

> *May I forgive those who have harmed me,*
> *either intentionally or unintentionally.*
> *May I be forgiven by those who I have harmed,*
> *either intentionally or unintentionally.*
> *May I forgive myself for the times I have harmed myself,*
> *either intentionally or unintentionally.*

Forgiveness gives you permission to start anew. It opens the heart to new and loving choices. To integrate forgiveness with loving-kindness, see Practice/Meditation #44 and #100.

95

DEPARTURE

Mindfully Aid Digestion After Eating

To eat is human; to digest, divine.
—Charles T. Copeland

Have you noticed that the only time you think about your digestion is when it is not working optimally? It does not seem fair that eating gets all the glory while digestion does all the work.

What foods are difficult for you to digest? If you continue to consume such foods, you might ask why? Another good mindful digestion practice is to be aware of what you drink during and after the meal. How does this affect your digestion?

In traditional Chinese and eastern medicine, hot water and hot herbal teas—including ginger tea—are thought to enhance the power of digestive juices, as well as soothe one's temperament. On the contrary, iced drinks consumed at mealtime are believed to have the opposite effect of dampening the power of digestive juices. By paying greater attention, you can make choices that enhance the digestive process.

PRACTICE/MEDITATION

Today's mindful eating practice consists of exploring ways to improve digestion. Many people have trouble digesting lactose, gluten and other substances. It can help to keep a journal of those foods that your body has a problem with, as well as those that help it digest and function properly. Working with a registered dietitian or medical professional can help identify food issues, in addition to offering solid guidance regarding alternatives.

As mentioned previously, a soothing cup of tea makes a nice transition into what comes after your meal. Some studies also show that tea may also benefit and stimulate the immune system. Whether you are alone or with others, you can try different teas to explore their effect on your digestion and mood.

One caveat for drinking tea in the evening is that while many herbal teas have very little caffeine, some black and green teas have enough caffeine to negatively impact your sleep. The amount of caffeine in tea depends on the product's origin and preparation, so read the fine print. (Some tea can contain as much or more caffeine than coffee.)

In addition, be aware of the effects of excessive fluids and alcohol on digestive and other bodily processes. For example, the Mayo Clinic (mayoclinic.org) warns that "Regular consumption of more than two alcoholic drinks a day increases the risk of osteoporosis." As always, it is helpful to seek out professional or medical help when making dietary changes.

96

DEPARTURE

Leftovers for Food Lovers

Garbage becomes rose.
Rose becomes compost—
Everything is in transformation.
Even permanence is impermanent.
—Thich Nhat Hanh

Leftovers at mealtime are actually a starting point for transformation. For some, leftovers are predestined for the garbage, something worthless to be discarded. For others, leftovers represent a transformation into a meaningful treasure to be used another day. It seems that people either love leftovers or hate them.

After a meal, what do you do with your leftovers? Do you consistently eat more than you want to avoid leftovers, and then feel guilty about overeating? Do you cringe at the idea of reheated food? Or, do you find ways of combining leftovers to make a new and unique meal?

Even if you cannot stand to eat leftovers, you can still find a way to offer the food to others. A gift of food to another is almost always appreciated with love and joy.

§

PRACTICE/MEDITATION

Today's meditation is a reflection on the magical and transformative nature of food.

Find a quiet place to sit, noticing your breath and feeling the position of your body on the chair and your feet on the floor or ground. Now, for a moment, reflect on impermanence. Impermanence really means that over time, things change. The chair you sit in right now, for instance, was once in the form of a tree or minerals from the earth. The water flowing in a river and lake was once a cloud. Look at the room or environment around you, and imagine how many things have changed and transformed in the past 100 years.

Now, reflect on today's meal. It goes from being something that is separate from you before the meal into something that is part of you after the meal. This miracle is part of the continuing lesson on transformation that you—and all persons—receive through food and eating. Since food becomes part of *you*, does it not also follow that you become part of *it*? It is critical that you understand this, because food can directly affect moods and the way you feel.

Lastly, reflect on how you could transform leftovers into a gift for others. How would this change your relationship with the world around you? How affirming!

97

DEPARTURE

Leave the "Shoulds" and Blame Behind

Ego is not sin.
Ego is not something that you get rid of.
Ego is something that you come to know.
—Pema Chödrön, *Start Where You Are*

Have you ever mentally and emotionally beaten yourself up after a meal? If so, the chances are your statements fall into one of several ego blaming categories.

Firstly is guilt: "I *shouldn't* have eaten that extra helping." This has sometimes been called "shoulding" all over oneself. Secondly is seeing your eating patterns as all-or-none: "I'll *never* have control over my eating," or "I'll *always* be overweight." Thirdly is emotional overload, which could sound like: "I'm so *upset* that I can't stay on a healthy eating plan anyway." Is it really true that you *never* have control over your eating or that you *never* make a healthy food choice?

A better way to know yourself is not by giving credence to that blaming voice in your head, but by stepping back and reframing your thoughts and beliefs. There is always another side to every picture.

PRACTICE/MEDITATION

Today's after-meal practice focuses on reframing thoughts and emotions using a mindfulness perspective.

After transitioning out of your meal—by taking a short walk or enjoying a cup of tea as suggested earlier—find a quiet place where you can sit without interruption. Bring your full presence to any thoughts or feelings you are still having regarding the past meal.

Here, you will reframe and examine the nature of those feelings and thoughts as impermanent and transitory—as explored in Practice/Meditation #96. You might picture these thoughts as clouds passing by in the sky or as leaves floating down a stream. They are here for a passing moment, before moving past and disappearing.

When a thought or distraction captures your attention, that's okay. Just notice each new thought (or passing cloud) with a sense of neutrality, just like an objective witness might. No matter how many thoughts grab you, you can always come back home to the body and the breath by sensing each in-breath and out-breath and your body on the chair.

As you take your next breath, ask yourself this question: "This breath that I'm experiencing right now—is this yesterday or tomorrow?"

A mindfulness reframe helps you recognize that while thoughts can sometimes be useful, *they can be limiting and do not define you.* The present moment overflows with abundance. How spacious!

98

DEPARTURE

Be G.L.A.D. During and After the Meal

Live in simple faith . . .
Just as this
trusting cherry
flowers, fades, and falls.
—Issa, poet

H ave you ever said a heartfelt "thank you" to friends for inviting you to their home for dinner? You can think of it as a kind of departure blessing. This is a good way to transition from mealtime into what comes next.

In some cultures and traditions this departure is formalized. The Sabbath, for example, is sometimes concluded with the sweet smell of nutmeg and other spices—which represents hope for the week ahead. How can you depart your meal with a sense of optimism, hope, and faith? First, take a moment of pause to appreciate the meal you have just finished. You are the beautiful flower that has just been watered and nourished by your meal.

PRACTICE/MEDITATION

This practice will focus on departing your meal with gratitude. For using gratitude as a ritual, see Practice/Meditation #27.

With gratitude, you selectively attend to the good, the decent, the beautiful, the joyful things that life offers. Gratitude harnesses your attention in a way that nourishes and connects you with others. By doing this, gratitude engages you with life not as a passive viewer, but as an active participant.

1) **Basic Gratitude** includes things like water, food, warmth, shelter, and clothing. Without these, life would be unbearable or impossible.

2) **Ordinary Gratitude** consists of the myriad of little things for which we could be thankful, such as enjoying a cup of tea or coffee, a favorite book, the touch of a cooling breeze, and so on.

3) **Personal Gratitude** highlights all of the things that meaningfully contribute to your life, such as having transportation, a livelihood, good health, and so on.

4) **Relationship Gratitude** features the friends, family, pets and others who enrich your life with joy, laughter and companionship.

5) **Paradoxical Gratitude** means being thankful for those things you wish you *didn't* have in your life. Sometimes, those unwanted or unwelcome events can provide a surprising silver lining or a valuable life lesson that may help you in the future.

As you sit, notice as many different flavors of gratitude as you can from your mealtime. Share your findings with others as a way to keep gratitude in memory. How does it feel to reflect on gratitude in this way? How might you continue to use this practice?

99
DEPARTURE

Embrace Periodic Fasting Between Meals

If you let go a little,
you will have a little happiness.
If you let go a lot
you will have a lot of happiness.
If you let go completely
you will be free.
—Achaan Chah, Buddhist monk

When you depart from mealtime, do you still think about food, or maybe even plan and obsess over your upcoming meal? If you are on a diet regimen, for example, you may still be hungry or feeling unsatisfied. Or, perhaps you are thinking about how to do a better job of sticking to your dietary needs at the next meal. Whatever may be the case, my suggestion is as follows: Instead of living in the past or the future, consciously *embrace* this now moment of *non-eating*. Sometimes it is easier to let go of something if you proactively replace it with a potent substitute.

PRACTICE/MEDITATION

For this practice, you will reframe how you think about the time between your last meal and the next one. Instead of refraining from food until your next meal—which feels like you're giving something up—you can actively and intentionally choose non-eating as a choice.

The word intention has been used frequently in these pages. One way to think of intention is to view it as a vow. Vows are often public statements that declare your feelings and values—such as a wedding vow. But vows can also be understood as a statement of one's discipline and desire to do something worthwhile or to achieve a goal.

Intention goes beyond the idea of "trying" to do something. You might say, "I'll try not to each or nibble between meals." That's very different from saying, "I'm setting the intention to let my body rest and be free from eating and digesting until my next meal."

You could also consider the space between meals as a periodic, or temporary fast, which has many benefits. As used in many traditions, periodic fasting gives your entire body a rest.

An intention or vow to keep your periodic fast until the next meal strengthens both concentration and conviction. That is not to say, however, that you should be rigid with this vow. Even in the monastery, for example, although we took a vow not to eat after 12 noon, the monks were welcome to have tea or juice in the afternoon in case they needed it.

100

DEPARTURE

Light the Candle of Loving-Kindness

Better to light a candle than to curse the darkness.
—Confucius

You might want to think of your emotions and struggles that you hold onto after your meal as "darkness." But the moment you recognize the truth of how these various feelings push and pull at you, you have lit a "candle" that brings light into your life.

You do not need to depart your meal with emotional angst, frustration, and conflict over what you did or did not eat. You do not need to carry the calorie count with you as a reminder that weighs you down. Rather, accept these thoughts for what they are: one limited view of things at this moment.

The truth is that you are worthy of love. Love is the light that can dissolve the shadows and dark feelings. The timeless loving-kindness meditation, which was explained in Practice/Meditation #44 as a way of preparing a meal with love and care, is always appropriate for inviting the light of self-acceptance and self-love.

PRACTICE/MEDITATION

The loving-kindness meditation frees you from being weighed down from those times where you feel rejected, unhappy, or unloved—whether food-related or not. Research has shown that this ancient 2,500 year old practice primes us for feelings of safety and security. Even if you don't feel worthy of love, you can imagine saying the words here to the small child you once were.

To begin, find a quiet place where you can get settled in with your breath and body. If you want, you can start with forgiveness as described in Practice/Meditation #94.

Now, visualize those who care about you sending you the following words. You can say the words to yourself either out loud or inwardly. Even if you don't feel deserving of love, imagine saying these words to the small child you once were.

May I be well.
May I be happy and healthy.
May I be at peace.
May I be free from pain, hunger, and suffering.

Keep repeating these words to yourself as many times as necessary. *Also, feel free to adapt these words to best fit you.* For example, you could say, "May I be accepted, understood, welcomed, affirmed." Absorb these sentiments into your entire being. How healing!

101

DEPARTURE

Eat Your Meal in Reverse

Life can only be understood backwards,
but it must be lived forwards.
—Søren Kirkegaard, Danish philosopher

It is a paradox that your mind can hold on to that last meal while you are moving forward in time and space. But it's probably no surprise, especially if you exit the dinner table feeling bloated and heavy. How you feel after a meal can be a clue about whether you ate too much.

However, since life must be lived in the present moment, the choice to let go of the past makes good sense. Oddly, there may be another option if you have trouble releasing the emotions surrounding mindless eating.

The unusual answer may be to try what the philosopher Kirkegaard suggested: You can always play mealtime events in reverse motion. Playing them in reverse may help you discover the intense feelings that you tried to bury or forget with food. Though a reversal may seem difficult, it offers an intriguing way to put things in a fresh perspective.

PRACTICE/MEDITATION

For this meditation, you will replay a mindless meal in reverse. Pick a mindless meal where you checked out and ate without regards to noticing flavors, slowing down, or paying the slightest attention to your body's hunger and satiety cues.

All is not lost. Retrieving those mindless moments means that a reverse meal make-over can show you a lot. After getting settled in and picking a meal, start from the point you left the meal, noticing how you felt in that moment. Anytime that you lose focus, take a nice breath and then continue reversing the meal.

Use slow, reverse motion to back up one moment at a time. In particular, observe and identify those moments where you lost mindful eating. Note the situation in detail. What were you thinking about, what was distracting or grabbing your attention that made you unable to notice your food. (Emotions, distractions and many things can cause mindless eating.)

When you find a moment of mindlessness, replay the scene with a more beneficial intention and choice. In other words, relive the moment with mindful awareness, where you make the choice you would have made if you were mindful! Notice how this more beneficial choice feels. When you finally reach the beginning of the meal, you will have re-created those mindless moments and replaced them with mindful ones.

Now, move forward to the present with a joyful heart, ready to make new mindful choices and not dwelling on the past. How liberating!

INDEX OF QUOTES

Quotes at the beginning of each entry in *Simply Mindful Meal by Meal* are referenced below. Unreferenced quotes are from the author's personal collection from a variety of sources but without specific information.

1.

Michael Cader with Debby Roth; eds., *Eat These Words* (New York: HarperCollins, 1991), 37.

2.

Brother Peter Reinhart, *Brother Juniper's Bread Book* (New York: Addison Wesley, 1991), 179.

3.

16th century tea master Rikyu

4.

Eckhart Tolle, *The Power of Now* (Novato, CA: New World Library, 1999), 71.

5.

M.J. Ryan, ed. *A Grateful Heart* (Berkeley: Conari Press, 1994), 36.

6.

Ronald D. Fuchs, ed., *You Said a Mouthful* (New York: St. Martin's Press, 1996), 59.

7.

Socrates

8.

Pema Chödrön, *Comfortable With Uncertainty* (Boston: Shambhala, 2002), 138.

9.

Donald Altman

10.

Sanaya Roman, *Spiritual Growth* (Tiburon, CA: H J Kramer Inc., 1989), 130.

11.

Matsuo Bashō, Japanese Poet

12.

Sanaya Roman, *Spiritual Growth* (Tiburon, CA: H J Kramer Inc., 1989), 204.

13.

Pema Chödrön, *Start Where You Are* (Boston: Shambhala, 1994), 34.

14.

Thomas Byrom, trans., *Dhammapada: Sayings of the Buddha* (Boston: Shambhala, 1993), 21.

15.

Boy George, as quoted in *The Oregonian*, August 22, 2003

16.

Jesus, *Matthew 4:4*

17.

Gopi Krishna, *Kundalini* (Boston: Shambhala, 1970), 89.

18.

Deepak Chopra, *The Seven Spiritual Laws of Success* (San Rafael, CA: Amber-Allen Publishing and New World Library), 1994, 49.

19.

Philosopher George Santayana, 1863-1952

20.

Groucho Marx

21.

Ted Perry, *how can one sell the air?* (Summertown, TN: The Book Publishing Co., 1992), 47.

22.

Abraham Joshua Heschel, *The Sabbath* (New York: Noonday Press, 1975), 54.

23.

Deborah Kesten, *Feeding the Body, Nourishing the Soul* (Berkeley: Conari Press, 1997), 67.

24.

Dr. Vinod Verma, *Ayurveda for Life* (York Beach, ME: Samuel Weiser, Inc., 1997), 4

25.

Jesus, *Luke 11:9*

26.

Saint Benedict, *The Rule of St. Benedict* (Collegeville, MN: The Liturgical Press, 1982)

27.

M.J. Ryan, ed. *A Grateful Heart* (Berkeley: Conari Press, 1994), 163.

28.

Deepak Chopra, *The Seven Spiritual Laws of Success* (San Rafael, CA: Amber-Allen Publishing and New World Library, 1994), 73.

29.

Thomas Byrom, trans., *Dhammapada: Sayings of the Buddha* (Boston: Shambhala, 1993), 97.

30.

Gary W. Fenchuk, *Timeless Wisdom* (Midlothian, VA: Cake Eaters, Inc., 1998), 27.

31.

Kakuzo Okakura, *The Book of Tea* (Boston: Shambhala, 1993), 93-94.

32.

Ken McLeod, *Wake Up to Your Life* (San Francisco: HarperSanFrancisco, 2001), 411.

33.

Father Thomas Keating, *Open Mind, Open Heart* (NY: Continuum, 1992), 35.

34.

Ronna Kabatznick, Ph.D., *The Zen of Eating* (New York: A Perigee Book, 1998), 103.

35.

Gary W. Fenchuk, *Timeless Wisdom* (Midlothian, VA: Cake Eaters, Inc., 1998), 191.

36.

Charles Tart, *Living the Mindful Life* (Boston: Shambhala Publications, 1994), 41.

37.
Sara Sviri, *The Taste of Hidden Things* (Inverness, CA: The Golden Sufi Center, 1997), 44.
38.
Maria Polushkin Robbins, ed., *The Cook's Quotation Book* (Wainscott, NY: Pushcart Press, 1983), 22.
39.
Eckhart Tolle, *Stillness Speaks* (Novato, CA: New World Library, 2003), 7.
40.
Lama Surya Das
41.
Traditional Christian Grace
42.
Brother Rick Curry, *The Secrets of Jesuit Breadmaking* (New York: Perennial Press, 1995).
43.
Kalu Rinpoche, *The Dharma* (New York: State University of New York Press, 1986), 83.
44.
Sharon Tyler Herbst, *Never Eat More Than You Can Lift* (New York: Broadway Books, 1997), 96.
45.
Thelma Hall, *Too Deep for Words* (New York: Paulist Press, 1988), 32.
46.
Soei Yoneda, *Good Food from the Japanese Temple* (Tokyo: Kodansha International, 1982).
47.
Donna Schaper, *Sabbath Keeping* (Boston: Cowley Publications, 1999), 9.
48.
Zen Master Dogen, *From the Zen Kitchen to Enlightenment* (New York: Weatherhill, Inc., 1983), 7.
49.
Shakti Gawain, *Creative Visualization* (New York: Bantam, 1982), 37-38.
50.
A. M. Allchin and Esther de Waal, eds., *Daily Readings from Prayers and Praises in the Celtic Tradition* (Springfield, IL: Templegate Publishers, 1986), 27.
51.
M.J. Ryan, ed. *A Grateful Heart* (Berkeley: Conari Press, 1994), 219.
52.
The Buddha
53.
Saint Francis, *A Simple Prayer*
54.
Christopher Wormell, ed., *Kitchen Wisdom* (Philadelphia: Running Press, 1995),114.
55.
Eckhart Tolle, *The Power of Now* (Novato, CA: New World Library, 1999), 100.
56.
Kakuzo Okakura, *The Book of Tea* (Boston: Shambhala, 1993), 115.

57.

Gary W. Fenchuk, *Timeless Wisdom* (Midlothian, VA: Cake Eaters, Inc., 1998), 191.

58.

Soshitsu Sen XV, *Tea Life, Tea Mind* (New York: Weatherhill, 1979), 79.

59.

Sarah E. Parvis, ed., *The Quotable Feast* (Kansas City: Andrews McMeel, 2001), 4.

60.

Pema Chödrön, *Start Where You Are* (Boston: Shambhala, 1994), 26.

61.

Donald Altman, *Art of the Inner Meal* (Portland: Moon Lake Media, 2002), 82.

62.

Elizabeth Roberts and Elias Amidon, eds., *Prayers for a Thousand Years* (San Francisco: HarperSanFrancisco, 1999), 30.

63.

Philip Zaleski & Paul Kaufman, *Gifts of the Spirit* (San Francisco: HarperSanFrancisco, 1998), 117.

64.

Philip Zaleski & Paul Kaufman, *Gifts of the Spirit* (San Francisco: HarperSanFrancisco, 1998), 124.

65.

Andrew Weil, M.D., *Spontaneous Healing* (New York: Ballantine, 1996), 36.

66.

Annemarie Colbin, *Food and Healing* (New York: Ballantine, 1996), 23.

67.

Saint Benedict, *The Rule of St. Benedict* (MN: The Liturgical Press, 1982), 57.

68.

Venerable U Silananda

69.

Joseph Campbell, *The Power of Myth* (New York: Anchor Books, 1991), 30.

70.

Philip Zaleski & Paul Kaufman, *Gifts of the Spirit* (San Francisco: HarperSanFrancisco, 1998), 44.

71.

Luke 10:25

72.

Kate Rowinski, ed., *The Quotable Cook* (New York: The Lyons Press, 2000), 142.

73.

Ronna Kabatznick, Ph.D., *The Zen of Eating* (NY: Perigee, 1998), 51.

74.

David Scott and Tony Doubleday, *The Elements of Zen* (New York: Barnes & Noble Books, 1992), 61.

75.

The Dalai Lama, *Transforming the Mind* (London: Thorsons, 2000), 76.

76.

From a prayer service at Mount Calvary Monastery

77.

Krishnamurti, *Think On These Things*, (New York: HarperPerennial, 1989), 201-202.

78.

George Carlin, from Internet letter attributed to him.

79.

Compiled by Pat Rodegast and Judith Stanton, *Emmanuel's Book* (New York: Bantam, 1985), 102.

80.

Greg Johanson and Ron Kurtz, *Grace Unfolding* (New York: Bell Tower, 1991), 75.

81.

Michael Cader with Debby Roth; eds., *Eat These Words* (New York: HarperCollins, 1991), 57.

82.

William Bridges, *The Way of Transition* (Cambridge: Perseus Publishing, 2001),14.

83.

Thich Nhat Hanh, *Our Appointment With Life* (Berkeley, Parallax Press, 1990), 29.

84.

Maria Polushkin Robbins, ed., *The Cook's Quotation Book* (Wainscott, NY: Pushcart Press, 1983), 22.

85.

Compiled by Jack Kornfield and Paul Breiter, *A Still Forest Pool* (Wheaton, Il.: Quest Books, 1985), 70.

86.

Deepak Chopra, *The Seven Spiritual Laws of Success* (San Rafael, CA: Amber-Allen Publishing and New World Library, 1994), 53.

87.

William Bridges, *The Way of Transition* (Cambridge: Perseus Publishing, 2001), 16.

88.

Philip Zaleski & Paul Kaufman, *Gifts of the Spirit* (San Francisco: HarperSanFrancisco, 1998), 40.

89.

Huntington & Smith, eds., *Emerson Day by Day* (NY: Crowell & Co., 1905), 1.

90.

Jack Kornfield, *A Path with Heart* (New York: Bantam Books, 1993), 164.

91.

Sharon Tyler Herbst, *Never Eat More Than You Can Lift* (New York: Broadway Books, 1997), 140.

92.

Deepak Chopra, *Overcoming Addictions* (New York: Three Rivers Press, 1997), 109.

93.

Chef Bill Wavrin in *Chile Pepper* magazine, October 2003, p. 34.

94.

Father Thomas Keating, *Open Mind, Open Heart* (New York: Continuum Publishing Co., 1992), 17.

95.

Maria Polushkin Robbins, ed., *The Cook's Quotation Book* (Wainscott, NY: Pushcart Press, 1983), 68.

96.

Allan Hunt Badiner, ed., *Dharma Gaia* (Berkeley, CA: Parallax Press, 1990), 196.

97.

Pema Chödrön, *Start Where You Are* (Boston: Shambhala, 1994), 47.

98.

M.J. Ryan, ed. *A Grateful Heart* (Berkeley: Conari Press, 1994), 156.

99.

Jack Kornfield, *The Art of Forgiveness, Lovingkindness, and Peace* (New York, Bantam Books, 2002).

100.

Confucius

101.

Søren Kirkegaard

BOOKS BY DONALD ALTMAN

From the Simply Mindful Book Series

Simply Mindful Meal by Meal

Simply Mindful Resilience

Simply Mindful: A 7-Week Course and Personal Handbook

Simply Mindful Coloring Book

Travelers, a Novel

The Mindfulness Toolbox

One Minute Mindfulness

Clearing Emotional Clutter

The Mindfulness Code

Art of the Inner Meal

Living Kindness

The Mindfulness Toolbox for Relationships

Reflect: Awaken to the Wisdom of the Here and Now

The Joy Compass

Eat, Savor, Satisfy: 12-Weeks to Mindful Eating

NOTE FROM DONALD ALTMAN

Thank you for purchasing *Simply Mindful Meal by Meal*. I hope you enjoyed reading it and using the practices as much as I did writing it. If you have a few moments, please add a review to your favorite sites.

If you are interested in learning more about my work, sign up for my newsletter at: www.mindfulpractices.com

In Gratitude, Donald

Made in the USA
Las Vegas, NV
02 January 2025

15687743R00134